PEDAGOGY FOR MINISTERS

PEDAGOGY FOR MINISTERS

AN APPLICATION OF PEDAGOGICAL PRINCIPLES TO THE PREACHING AND OTHER WORK OF THE PASTOR

BY

ALVAH SABIN HOBART

Professor New Testament Interpretation in Crozer Theological Seminary
Author of "Seed Thoughts for Right Living," "Transplanted Truths from
Ephesians," "The Holy Spirit, Our Silent Partner," Etc.

NEW YORK   CHICAGO   TORONTO
Fleming H. Revell Company
LONDON   AND   EDINBURGH

New York: 158 Fifth Avenue
Chicago: 17 N. Wabash Ave.
Toronto: 25 Richmond St., W.
London: 21 Paternoster Square
Edinburgh: 100 Princes Street

PREFACE

SOME years ago a school-teacher friend of mine led me to make a study of pedagogy. As a science it was all new to me. In my college days there was no such study in the curriculum. I found the science so full of interest and practical usefulness in my preaching that when I took my place as a teacher of young ministers I, on my own initiative, undertook to give as an elective some lectures upon it. So many expressions came to me appreciative of the study that I have been led to put a condensation of those lectures into this form for the benefit of the hundreds of men in our correspondence course, and for such other men as have not had the benefit of such study. It is, as will be seen, not technical. It is suggestive only. If the " seed catches," as the farmers say, it will make the lawn green.

A. S. H.

Crozer Theological Seminary.

CONTENTS

I

Go ye, therefore, and make disciples of all nations; baptizing them into the name of the Father, and of the Son and the Holy Spirit.—
MATT. 28:19.

THE PASTOR AN EDUCATOR

MR. SPURGEON once said that he could not talk on any public occasion without a text. If he did not have one stated he had one in mind. The text controlling my thought in these chapters reads as follows:

Go ye, therefore,

Disciple all nations.

Baptizing them in the name of the Father, and of the Son, and of the Holy Spirit.

Teaching them to observe all things whatsoever I commanded you.

And lo, I am with you always even unto the end of the world.

This commission, whether it was given at that time or gathered after the ascension, as some think, from the tenor of his teachings and summed up in this form, is the most important of Christian teaching next to the promise of salvation by faith in Jesus.

It not only was necessary for their guidance,

since he left the whole cause for which he came into the world in their hands, but it was necessary for their encouragement in the arduous undertaking. If they had not done what this directed them to do the message and the teaching of Jesus would have evaporated from men's minds in a generation or two and made no considerable mark upon the world's life.

But because they sought to obey the command, and to pass it on to others, and because the churches also have ever since taken it as their commission, the Gospel has been preached, and the truth has been taught to a great portion of the world.

And since the pastors are the natural inheritors of the commission it is in an especial degree incumbent on them to give attention to the full import of the commission.

It has four consecutive steps.

"*Go.*" It is not "stay and give the gospel to all that come," but *go* to all. "Disciple" all nations. That included what Paul said he was especially told to do. (Rom. 1 : 5, 10 : 14, 15; Gal. 1 : 16.)

It was what the twelve did not attempt to do very enthusiastically. Peter needed to be taught it again when he was sent to Cornelius. (Acts 10 : 1-48.) The whole church in Jerusalem needed to have it pressed upon them after Peter had been taught it. Nearly all Jerusalem Christians had

failed to see the full import of it, and it took per-
secution to scatter them before they were able to
see it as a duty to " speak the word to the Gentiles also " (Acts 11 : 19-21) and persuade them
to enroll in the school of Jesus as " disciples " or
students.

" *Baptize.*"   That is lead them out into a public
confession in the appointed way.

" *Teach* " them.   After they are enrolled in the
school of Jesus do not think that all is now done;
that now they are " saved "; as if salvation meant
only some sort of insurance against future punishment, but give them the enlightenment and discipline of life that will lead them to do what Jesus
had taught that men ought to do to " *observe
whatsoever I have commanded you.*"

This " *teaching* them to observe " is to crown
your endeavors.   It is to be the goal to which you
are to try and bring them all.   It is the dominating purpose that should regulate and infuse itself
into all your other work.

We do not have the record of the actual work
of those twelve.   But we have the record which
makes it certain that they learned well the meaning of the commission, for they and the first generation of believers preserved in the gospels the
teaching of Jesus.   Both by recorded word and
by the example of the Lord himself we are freed
from doubt concerning what sort of lives he desires us to live.

Consider then the importance that is attached to teaching.

In the Old Testament Moses was a great teacher. (Deut. 4:1.) "And now O Israel hearken unto the statutes and unto the ordinances that I teach you, to do them; that ye may live, and go in and possess the land which Jehovah, the God of your fathers, giveth you." This Moses has been the most influential of all the men of history except the Man of Nazareth. Mosaic ideas of justice and mercy, of truth and fidelity to duty, of courage and patience saturate the practices of all the Christian and Mohammedan world.

When Samuel came to the leadership of Israel he said to them: "Far be it from me that I should sin against Jehovah in ceasing to pray for you, but I will instruct you in the good and right way."

Elisha appears to have been at the head of a school for the prophets. (II Kings 2:3-7; 4:1; 5:22; 9:1.)

Job said of God, Who is a teacher like unto him? (36:22.) See also 35:11.

The Psalms abound in allusions to the teaching of truth.

"Jehovah will instruct sinners in the way." (25:8.) "Come ye children hearken unto me, I will teach you the fear of the Lord." (Ps. 34:11.)

"Restore unto me the joy of thy salvation then will I teach transgressors thy ways and sinners shall be converted unto thee." (Ps. 51:13.)

"So teach us to number our days that we may get a heart of wisdom." (Ps. 90:12.) (See also 94:12.)

A study of the Psalms shows that all the fundamental principles of education were employed by those who arranged the liturgical services of the temple. There is a rich amount of song in which the character of God is declared. There are songs of praise from the men of great faith. There are warnings against wickedness. The grandest metaphors and the finest of similes are used to express good men's ideas of God. Then there are the historical psalms like the 104-106, in which the history of the nation as God had guided it was taught by oft repetition. In all this the purpose was not simply to tell the story of the nation but to show that God's hand was in it all. Merle d'Aubigné wrote in the preface of his history of the Reformation, " The history of the world should be set forth as the annals of the Sovereign king." . . . " I have gone down the lists whither the recitals of our historians have invited me. There I have witnessed the actions of men, and of nations, developing themselves with energy, and contending in violent collision. I have heard a strange din of arms, but I have nowhere seen the majestic countenance of the presiding Judge."

That could not be said of the Bible. It sketches

the path along which the nation of Israel stumbled; but the hand of God is in every leading event, and the guidance of God in every great man's life. The historical books and the devotional books alike are books that teach the things of God and the duties of man. Even the outbursts of praise from joyous souls, and the mournful cries of men in great trial, were sought out and inserted in the book to teach the way of God with men. The charge of d'Aubigné against modern historians cannot be brought against the men who wrote or the men who sorted out from the writings the books that make our Bible. In that Book the "majestic countenance of the judge" always shines upon the path of the people who worship him.

In the New Testament. Here the record shows that Jesus' great work was teaching. (Matt. 7:29.) We read that he "taught them as one having authority." (Mark 10:1.) "The multitudes came together and as he was accustomed he taught them."

(John 7:14) "He went into the temple and taught."

(John 3:2) When Nicodemus came to talk with him he said, "We know that thou art a teacher come from God."

And these verbal designations are only indications of what is in the heart of all his ministry. He was always teaching men the things of God.

All Jerusalem and all Galilee thought of him not as some great, fiery orator, like John the Baptist, nor like the prophet Elijah, but as a man who was stirring up the country by his teaching. He set men to thinking. When he rebuked he showed them why they deserved his rebukes. When he exhorted he gave them reasons for his exhortation. When he would inspire them to courage and endurance he gave the truth which was back of his encouragement. (John 18:37.) When he stood before Pilate and was asked if he were a king he replied, " I came into the world to bear witness to the truth."

After he was gone his disciples became teachers. The complaint made about them was (Acts 3:42): " These men, whom you had in prison, are ' standing and teaching the people.' " . . . " And every day they ceased not to teach and preach Jesus as the Christ." When the church was started at Antioch, Barnabas came and hunted up Saul who was then getting a great name as a teacher and " for a whole year taught much people." (Acts 11:26.)

Apollos was said to have " taught accurately the things concerning Jesus " but he was not fully informed. Then Aquila and Priscilla took him and " instructed him more perfectly." This seems to have been the first theological school after Jesus' ascension and a woman was one of the professors.

The nature of the work. Beyond all these exemplifications of the teaching habit of great leaders, and beyond all the suggestions that may come from the word "teacher" or "teaching," there lies in the very nature of the pastor's work the necessity for teaching. The pastor's work is to lead men to high moral and spiritual life. But that can only be done by enabling them to see and feel the truth that moral and spiritual life rest upon. Men may be scared into an outward conformity, but they are not transformed by it. Break a man's sense of fear and he will go back to his sins "as a sow to her wallowing in the mire." (James.) Men may be coaxed into joining a church to please friends or to gain some social end, but they are not lifted in their life. Men may be hired to join the procession of the Christian world by promises of heaven or something that they value more than heaven. Such are only a higher kind of "rice Christians."

All these fail when the times of trial come. But the man who has been made to see the truth that underlies all the Christian life is as sure to go the way of truth as water is to run down hill. Men cannot commit themselves, and they ought not to commit themselves, as the Christian must commit himself, either to a system of ethics or to a theory of life or to the man Jesus as Savior, unless they know enough about them to justify their faith. If they know but little they can trust but little. If they begin their discipleship upon an erroneous idea of what it means they will desert the cause when they discover their error. They must be taught the principles correctly.

It is the men who are convinced that stay in the line of duty. When men have begun correctly they must still be taught the truths adapted to maturer experience. If they have been mistaught they are to be corrected. As Paul wrote to Titus, they must be "convinced by sound doctrine." An incorrect doctrine will deflect a man's conduct as surely as a load of steel will deflect the needle of the ship's compass. One cannot hold a philosophy that is against the Christian teaching without his life being gradually deflected from the Christian path. A Utilitarian will find his estimate of conduct out of harmony with the estimate made by a man who is an Idealist. A Calvinistic theology will impart a tone to a man's life different from that which an Armenian theology will give. This is why Paul in his attempts to correct the life of the disciples began his letters with a doctrinal section and then from the doctrine he proceeded with his "Therefores" to specific lines of duty.

(Rom. 5:1) *Therefore* we have peace with God.

(Gal. 6:1) Stand fast *therefore* in the liberty wherewith Christ hath set us free.

(Eph. 4:1) I *therefore* beseech you to walk

worthy of the calling. Note the first words of nearly every chapter of Hebrews and see how the logical inference from the preceding truth is made toward a practical duty. Thus it appears that the teaching function of the pastor is not an incident but an essential element in his proper fulfilment of his high calling.

The pastor is a man who has been up into the high mountain of truth and seen the far-reaching landscape. He has found the path by which he can climb again. Then he comes down and leads his people up to where he has been. And when they have seen the vision from that viewpoint, they will never be the same people again. Some of the details will fade from the mind but there will be a residuum. The world will never be so small again. Life will never appear so short or so unimportant. The emotion may die out, the ambition of the hour may be satisfied, but the soul itself will remain larger and purer for the vision.

Teaching is the nearest to miracle-working of anything we can do. To give a man a clear idea of a great truth is to put something into his mind that will remake the whole man. History is full of instances in which a new view of the facts of life changed men so much that the words of the apostle are suitable, " They are begotten again by the word of truth."

Elijah's work was spectacular. His deeds seem like ancient marks of high water that we look at and wonder if the water ever was so high, and if it ever will be again. The Psalms are rippling streams of sparkling water inviting us to drink. Ezra no doubt did some good exhortation, but the work of which he has most reason to rejoice now is that he organized the temple services on a teaching basis, and wrought to secure a bible for the instruction of Israel.

The liturgies of the church are not only vehicles for the worshipping soul to express itself, but they are schools of instruction. Looking at the churches that we call strong churches—not large churches always—and we see that they have been the care of educational pastors. The men who are honored most among us all are men who have the teaching gift. I do not mean to say that "house going" pastors and "ingathering" pastors have little usefulness, for they are both useful and necessary; but I mean that the more permanent results are from the labors of those who have the teaching gift well exercised and developed.

Evangelism has a great place in the work of the kingdom. Mr. Moody, Elder Knapp, "Sam" Small, and "Sam" Jones, Dr. Finney, Gipsy Smith, Mr. Chapman, are names that will be remembered. But their work is scattered about and they cannot stay to conserve it. But F. W. Robertson, for example, had a work that remains. It has been written of him that "on those whose tendencies were toward skepticism the effect of his sermons was remarkable. " I never hear him," said one, " without some doubt being removed, or some difficulty being solved. Young men who had boasted publicly of doubts which were an inward terror to them could not resist the attractive power of his teaching, and fled to him to disclose the history of their hearts, and find sympathy and guidance." " The most visible part of his work was among working men. He bound fifteen hundred of them together in a bond of mutual helpfulness." " Dissenting preachers spoke of his sermons with praise. Business men wrote to say that they felt that Christianity was a power in life. Men whose intellect had been wearied with pulpit sameness read them with interest. Fourteen editions of his sermons have been printed and are yet read by many with profit."

Mr. Spurgeon was a great educator. Not only in his preaching did the teaching element abound but in his pastoral work and plans his college and his preachers' school were central. His work all has the earmarks of true pedagogy.

Mr. Beecher taught, but in his own peculiar way. He was so much of a student of psychology that he was an interpreter of men to themselves. He always based his sermons and his appeals on some common and familiar experience, and then started from that to practical inferences from the experience. His congregations were religiously well trained. And when he died, although they were thus made orphans, yet without a quaver the church went on with the work he had begun.

On the contrary Mr. Talmadge in the same city, at the same time, gathered great congregations and was a great pulpiteer. But when he was gone it took only a few weeks to disband the church. They had been accustomed to stare at his great stereopticon metaphors; they had revelled in his poetic fancies; but they had done no thinking on great problems and had no power to solve them.*

As a more recent instance we may name J. Campbell Morgan. Perhaps no man of equal ability in preaching mingles so much of the true teaching quality as he. Some of his views and of his interpretations may not meet with your approval, but his ability to impress them on his audiences is hardly equalled by any one.

* After writing the above the following editorial appeared in the *Watchman-Examiner:*
Dr. Talmadge was a pulpit orator of the flamboyant, sensational type. His sermons were not intended primarily for the edification or the comfort of a local congregation and were quite as applicable to the people of Kamchatka as to the people of Brooklyn. He had no personal touch with people of his congregation and no intimate knowledge of their needs or their aspirations. When the great Tabernacle went up in flames the church collapsed. In the great heterogeneous congregation there was not enough of energy and spiritual life to enable it to get together to erect a new house of worship; so the church went out of existence, and the members scattered to other congregations.

" The foremost thought of the ministry is responsibility for the oversight of souls, although that is blent, so that the two can hardly be kept apart, with the further task of religious instruction. . .. . The idea of stewardship in connection with the minister has special reference to providing the household with supplies of divine truth." (Oswald Dykes.)

" Commending ourselves in the sight of every man by the manifestation of the truth." (Paul.)

The teaching pastor, therefore, is in the best of company and has the surest, brightest prospects of long and unfailing usefulness.

I urge you to cultivate with all possible enthusiasm, care, and patience the teaching quality of your preaching. It will be the people whom you have " convinced by sound doctrine " who will stand by when the strain comes. Those whom you only please without edifying will hide when the storm arises. The young whom you educate will recall with gratitude your ministry. They will tell the children, " He is the man that showed me the truth. All that came afterwards only watered the flowers that he planted."

II.

WHAT IS PEDAGOGY?

IF we are to be teachers it will be well for us to think over the content of that word "teaching." We use it in the broad sense as the equivalent of "educating." And the science of educating is called the science of pedagogy. Primarily the word meant to lead the young. In the old Roman world the well-to-do sent a servant along with their young children to the school as a guard and guide. He was called a *pedagogue*. In the King James version of the Bible (Gal. 3:24) we read that "the law was a schoolmaster"— (in the Greek it is pedagogue)—"to lead us to Christ." But now we call pedagogy the science of teaching in any and in all grades. There is a branch of it in the primary and another in the intermediate departments. I am applying the word to some part of the preacher's activities.

General pedagogy is the science of leading out. Powers of body or mind that are latent are to be led out into full activity. For example, a man has by nature the gift of speech. But if it be

23

not led out—e-ducated—it will be a small affair.
It was said of Bismarck that he could be silent in
seven languages. Unless the gift of possible
speech with which we are endowed be cultivated
we shall practically be silent in every language.
Many a man comes into our classes who has ideas
and thinking powers of unusual value, but whose
power of speech is so poorly developed that his
ideas are shut up in his mind. He cannot give
them any adequate expression. They are of not
much more use in the world than the possible
statue of a great man that is contained in a block
of fine marble but not yet cut out.

All men have some imagination. But unless it
be developed a great part of the world's wisdom
and beauty will be—so far as such undeveloped
minds are concerned—as if they did not exist.
Men have reasoning powers, but how feeble they
are until they have been brought into fullness by
use. When they have been brought out into maturity man is put upon the throne that makes him
preëminent in creation. The animate and inani-
mate worlds submit to his dominance. So with
the moral powers. Reverence for God, respect for
one's self, love of truth for truth's sake, kindness
to our fellow men are embryonically present in
all, but they must be e-ducated until we are in
character Christ-like.

Take the case of men, we will say, who have
come into the church from some great evangelistic

meeting. They are real converts to Christ, but how embryonic they are! Their idea of God is that he is a great king. The words of the Psalm are suitable for them: " Jehovah is a God of gods." "Greatly to be feared is Jehovah in the assemblies of the saints." When they pray their prayers are a cross between children asking of their fathers and men begging favor of a tyrant. They are like Solomon at the dedication of the temple. He prayed repeatedly that Jehovah would hear the prayers of his people and when they turned from evil ways forgive them. One would think that Jehovah's readiness to forgive was a doubtful matter, and therefore Solomon needed to remind him of his duty in the case. But after a time these same men will have so far developed their sense of Jehovah's goodness that they almost cease to ask but only praise. As Dr. W. N. Clarke expressed it " such men do not think the Church is a widow but a bride, her Lord always at hand."

Here is a man with a large amount of good in him but only a little of the leaven of truth. After a time the leaven, under the influence of good teaching, works its wonderful changes so that he lives for great purposes and in great joyfulness.

This boy, just opening his eyes to the world, with every sensibility alert, making his life choices of companions and occupations and principles—

the teacher is to so direct him in these formative years that his future course will be one of wisdom and loyalty to Christ.

To educate, then, is much more than telling people something they did not know before you told them. That is only a small part of educating them. It must seek to give them power to find out things for themselves. To explain the Bible is good, but to give them power to explain it themselves is better.

It is more than to train men to certain lines of action. Dogs can be trained to do some things. I have seen statements that even fleas can be trained to do things. And one man has trained flies to perform tricks. Even pigs have been taught to pick out letters. And it is possible to train people to do what are called religious acts with about as much real intelligence about them as these other trained animals have in their doings. There are no thought processes set into motion. It is habit or memory or association only. These are all parts of education but they are only preliminary activities looking toward maturer developments.

Some pastors do a great amount of this training work. I knew of one who succeeded in getting more than fifty of his members to stand up and repeat the first eight chapters of Romans. That was a great success. But they may have gained only a very little idea of Paul's teaching after all. I knew a girl in the Sunday School who repeated several chapters from the book of John. But she was too young to have the faintest idea of what it was all about. That was good memory drill but it was not moral or religious education. One good man used to say he did not think he knew a passage of scripture until he had practiced it.

In the pastor's task therefore there is more than getting people to know the story of the Bible and the Creed and the Catechism. More than to secure an habitual attendance on the services of the church. He must bring out into full strength the latent spiritual forces and get them into action.

In religious matters it is more than mastering some of the problems of theology, important as those are. It is a sad fact that many who are experts in theology are perverts in practical life. We might at some time send a man from our school with a degree, of whom his fellow students think that another, whose scholarship scarcely warrants a diploma, is better educated in religion than he.

It is bringing social virtues to maturity. I do not mean the power of conversation, but I mean the ability and disposition to live in company with one's fellow men and do his part, carry his share of the burden, trust his fellows and be trusted by them. To put it concretely it means to be

a neighborly, law-obeying citizen who votes and
votes on the right side of great moral questions;
who pays his debts as promptly as he is able;
who pays his taxes without grumbling; who helps
others to do their duty. It means readiness to
do his part and pay his proportion in the church,
and not to be a crank.

*It is making the spiritual part of men to be-
come dominant.* They are to be led into such
an estimate of values that things of affection and
character are considered to be worth more than
things that can be eaten, or things that can be
counted and weighed. They are to be led to see
that things that have their beginning and end in
this world are of less importance than things of
eternity. And this means that what is called
spiritual life be not misunderstood. In my school
days I used, as students do now, go out here and
there to supply vacant pulpits. I thus had opportunity to hear many estimates of other preachers.
I found that in very many cases if a man preached
the severer side of the truth he was called an
" old-fashioned preacher." If he reasoned of righteousness in a modern way he was called a " doctrinal preacher "—" smart but not very pious."
If he was a teaching preacher they said, " That
man fed me. I can go like Elijah on the strength
of that meat forty days." But if he stirred the
emotions and made the congregation weep, they
said he was a " spiritual preacher." Each of

these characterizations contain a truth, but the really spiritual life is one that recognizes that God is a great person analogous to ourselves. And that we have a kind of intercourse with him.

Spiritual life is that set of feelings and activities that are produced in us by the thought that we are in the presence and under the care of that Great Person who is over all and is the Father of all. To think of ourselves in the presence of such a Person is to fill us with the noblest ambitions and inspire us with the greatest zeal for doing the things that are pleasing to him. All other activities are contributory to doing, feeling, and thinking his wishes for us.

It is a whole and not a fractional undertaking. The Evangelist is to do one kind of work. The Visitor another. But the Educator is charged with all these. He is the Captain-of-spiritual-industry. He is Commander-in-chief of the latent forces. He calls out all the reserves of the soul and directs them toward the welfare of the whole man. He is the Superintendent of a school.

My purpose is to apply these principles to all the work over which the pastor has oversight.

It will be considered first as pulpit pedagogy and then as administrative pedagogy.

Pulpit pedagogy. The principles are the same in pulpit pedagogy as those underlying all school work; but the circumstances make the application of them more complex. In school the teacher can ask questions, and can encourage questions; and thus be able to know the needs of the student. But in the pulpit work, there is no opportunity for questions and answers. The sermon must in some way meet the needs, and answer the questions that are not asked. It must be in many cases a one-sided dialogue answering in the sermon the questions that are only in the hearer's mind. It must also touch the springs of action so that the hearer will put into life what the preacher has put into the sermon. The study and the use of methods by which to accomplish these things is what may be called Pulpit pedagogy.

To be able to profit by such a study one needs to have some familiarity with the primary principles of psychology, and to be fairly well informed in school pedagogy for the principles are the same to considerable extent.

Great help can be gained by frequent visits to the public schools, or by acquaintance and conversation with public school teachers.

Valuable suggestions can also be gained by the study of the methods of those denominations that emphasize the teaching of the church more than the evangelistic duty. In that line their experience is a subject of profitable consideration. We may adopt without compunction the saying of Cromwell to his soldiers—(but we think in a much better cause and better spirit): " The earth is the Lord's and the fullness thereof. We are the Lord's people. Therefore help yourselves."

Administrative pedagogy. In the application of pedagogy to the larger part of the pastoral field the *need* for invention, and for the more subtle influence of pedagogy, is greatly felt. All the various departments of the pastor's activity require the guidance of this teaching purpose. In the Sunday School he will seek to foster the best grade of teaching. All his wit and wisdom will be needed. All his resources will be called upon there. Good teaching has to compete in the Sunday School with a whole battalion of brave competitors. They include the social demands of the day, class distinctions, the ties of good fellowship that bind the classes together, the craze for entertainment, the Boy Scout and the Campfire Girls' themes, not to mention the mission lessons, the lawn festivals, and, lately, the Red Cross gatherings; all of which seek discussion in the classes.

Each one of these is useful but the ability to conserve their good and to so direct them that they will work together toward true education along true pedagogical lines is a gift greatly to be desired and almost imperatively demanded.

In pastoral visitation the necessity to be so entertaining as to be welcome, and yet make visits to the family both welcome and useful, taxes the best powers of the pastor.

In the liturgical part of the services he has to struggle with titanic forces in the people who do not know what they come to church for, and with those who come for pious entertainment on a semi-pious holiday, and with the choir who want to make a good showing of their musical abilities, and with his own subtle ambition to commend himself as an " elegant sermonizer "—a maker of sermons having " artistic perfectness."

In the liturgical churches such as the Roman Catholic, Episcopalian, or Lutheran, the pastors are relieved in large measure of the responsibility of arranging the liturgy. It has all been arranged for them by councils of men who gave the best wisdom to its arrangement. But in the Baptist, Congregational, and in lesser degree the Presbyterian and Methodist churches the weight of responsibility is thrown upon the pastor. And he, in a great majority of cases, never has had any teaching or any study of the pedagogical intent or value of the liturgical part of the services.

As Dr. Oswald Dykes has said: " But where everything is left, as in Congregational and modern Presbyterian worship, to the minister as sole leader, his training for this high function has been notoriously and unaccountably neglected."

But in all these departments of his work there is both an opportunity and consequently an obligation to regulate all that is done by the best pedagogical principles and highest educational aims.

III.

*Paul standing on the stairs beckoned with his hand unto the people: and when there was a great silence he spake unto them in the Hebrew language saying, Brethren and fathers hear ye the defence which I now make unto you. And when they heard that he spake unto them in the Hebrew language they were the more quiet.—*ACTS 21:40.

ATTENTION

IN selecting from the principles of pedagogy those that are usable in the pulpit we come first to the matter of attention on the part of the congregation. No considerable influence can be exerted by a sermon that does not have the attention of the hearers. Here, as in teaching, that is first in time as well as in importance.

The preacher has difficulties in this connection that the teacher does not have. The parents send the children to school and to Sunday School, but they do not require them to attend church. The rewards for attendance and the cards for good lessons are not available for the preacher. He must both create, to some extent, the appetite and then furnish the food. In the class there is the opportunity to address a question to an inattentive scholar, and perhaps the teacher may even rebuke inattention. There is also the restraining and compelling influence of the teacher's nearness to each scholar in the class. These the preacher lacks.

On the other hand, there are avenues of approach open for the preacher that are closed to the teacher. The general atmosphere in the preacher's audience is one of quiet and attention, outward at least. And that is favorable. Then attention is based upon interests of many kinds. There are many avenues to interest open to the preacher that are not open to the teacher. And some of them will reach some of the hearers.

An incident in business, political, or social life is always an opening to interest. Just as most people want to have some human figure in the painting of a landscape, and feel that the picture is lonesome without it, so a sermon or a discussion of abstract truth is far less likely to interest than something that connects with people. If a preacher says, " There was a man," or, " We read yesterday such an such an incident," or, " If a man does so and so," at once he has the attention of every one. He may lose it if his story is not good, but he has interest at the start. Dr. John A. Broadus, the " prince of preachers," in the South once had a congregation of men who were in the habit of staying outside until after he had begun his sermon, and then come clumping along in over the uncarpeted floor with squeaky boots. He could not rebuke them nor ask them to do otherwise for they were of the extra independent breed of Baptist. But he took up the practice of beginning each sermon with a story of some sort. And in a little while they had the habit of coming in before the sermon began.

Attention may be gained by beauty of expression. A good woman once said to me: "Make your sermons beautiful. The truth is worthy of it." The cultivation of good rhetorical speech is a source of power. A young rhetorician in Milan, Italy, used to go to church to hear the preacher Ambrose. He did not care for the doctrine, but he was so delighted with the beautiful language of the preacher that he went with regularity. But in so doing he came to accept the Gospel, and became the great theologian Augustine.

A fine voice has great power to interest people. This is a resource that has not been given the attention it ought to have. A full sweet, clear voice that responds to every wave of emotion in the thought holds men, and they get the message thus spoken. It was the habit of Gerritt Smith to speak forty minutes every day, when he did not have an address to make, in order not to lose control of his voice. Men who at first were not disposed to agree with what he said would go long distances to hear him.

The appeal to curiosity is of great value. It has great value in other matters of which more will be said in a later chapter. But in this matter it has great utility. This may be invoked by the use of the question form. In the sermon one can describe a situation and then ask, What is the outcome of this. Taking things as we know them to be what is the right way to act under such circumstances? Or one may state a problem and ask, What is the word of Paul or of Jesus on this? Sometimes a pause before a statement will attract attention as they wait for the word. To delay the final statement by any process awakens curiosity and thus holds attention.

Some men gain attention by using unique and grotesque metaphors, and somewhat startling phrases. "Billy" Sunday has that power to the utmost limit. If he did not have he could not hold his audiences. A large part of them go to hear his vivid, and often ludicrous characterizations of men and things. It is a great power. One need not attempt imitation of his phrases, but it is worth while to cultivate striking ways of saying things; and to state all religious truths in phrases that are transparent to the hearers. To preach in the vernacular may crucify a man's literary pride, but sermons of that sort will not crucify so much the time and feelings of the hearers as those sermons do that are so elegant as to lose their pungency. Mr. Spurgeon used to say, "Polish your sword but do not round the edge in doing so."

Illustrations are a great source of interest. If

they are really illustrations and not mere stories, they do a double duty. They fix attention and they convey truth to the heart.

A great inclusive requirement is that *the preacher have a message which he wants to give the congregation for their benefit, and is dead in earnest about it.* Earnestness is a contagious thing. We often hear men approve a preacher because " he is so earnest." " He seems to be so sincere," they say.

Margaret Slattery says, " Given well-prepared material, in which one is interested heart and soul, and the problem of gaining attention is half solved."

The man behind the sermon speaks through the sermon. " The real power of your oratory," said Bishop Brooks, " must be your own intelligent delight in what you are doing." " To be dead in earnest is to be eloquent." " The preacher's personal interest is the buoyant air that fills the mass and lifts it."

These things of which I have been speaking are important details of the work but not its central, vital part. As the painter must have the technique of his art or he cannot give expression to his ideals, so the preacher may not be ignorant nor careless in matters of technique, although it remains true that " a living dog is better than a dead lion." A sermon full of life and blunders is better than one empty of both.

Art is for the sake of the sermon, not the sermon for the sake of the art.

But there are some elements for the lack of which none of these things I have mentioned can make amends.

In the heart of all these things there must be some truth worth knowing. Henry Ward Beecher's father was once asked how he got the attention of his audience. He replied, " Give them something to attend to." That is a vital element. Sermons must have some real worthy content. It need not be information or reasoning. It may be exhortation or evangelism. But it must have some worthy thing in mind or no sort of approach to men's minds will hold attention long.

The hearer has a right to expect some return for his time and attention. If his return is not satisfactory he will mentally be away on other errands of thought. A school superintendent once said to a preacher, " You disturb my thoughts. I am accustomed to have my own thoughts when the sermon is going on." Thoughts ought to be " disturbed." There is no good reason for men to sit through a sermon just as a matter of respect for the preacher.

One must have a purpose and be moving toward its accomplishment.

It is easier to get attention than to hold it. The minds of a congregation of common people are not used to continued attention. The speaker can hold them for a few minutes around one idea, then he will find them becoming less attentive. If he can now pass to some other phase of the subject he gets a new point of interest and they will concentrate upon that for a time. So by changing the viewpoint he can hold their minds during the whole discourse. But these separate points must have a connection with each other such that they are parts of a whole. When one is dropped the mind should be left at the very door of the next one. But there must be something more than a series of points all on a level, and unconnected. These points must have a forward and an upward movement.

A New England deacon said about his pastor, " His sermons are like the clouds in June. They are always moving on." If a sermon only chases itself around like a dog chasing its tail one may smile at it for a little but interest soon evaporates. Try and accomplish something in a sermon and make everything bend toward that aim, and it will be recognized and listened to.

And what is true of the progressive arrangement is true also of the persuasive element. To give the best persuasives and the most emotional at the first makes the sermon an anticlimax. All the latter part will be a disappointment. Both the persuasive and the pedagogical parts should move upward as well as onward. There should be a sort of transfiguration effect such that men will

feel when they go from church that they have
come down from a mountain. Though the immediate sense of glory will lessen, the effect will
not evaporate.

A "skeleton" is important; that is, an orderly and logical arrangement of the several
parts. I am not intending to belittle the preachers who have little if any analytical ability. Some
of them have a good spirit and say many good
things. They get large congregations. They are
magnetic speakers who call men together, and it
does men good to get together even if they only
get a pious entertainment. They do get much
more. But as educators these men must take a
second place in comparison with those men who
have the logical and analytical faculty better
developed.

Without knowing it, all men have a logical
sense. All men think logically if they think at
all. Indeed Logic is not a set of rules imposed
on men for their thinking. Logic is only an
orderly exposition of the way that men do think.
If a man's sermon follows the truly natural order
most of his hearers will follow and find help without discovering that there was any logic about it.
But there are some who are logical consciously.
They test a man's sermons by rules. They detect
any failure to make his conclusions clear or certain. For such the preacher must try to fit his
discourse. If he has a "skeleton" and follows it

he will hold their attention and gain their respect for his teaching.

To make this "skeleton" requires care and study. Phillips Brooks used to sketch in brief the suggestions for the various points of his sermon. He assigned about so many pages for one point and so many for another. Then he arranged them in logical order. After that he wrote out in full, being careful not to have more than thirty pages of manuscript. The "Life and Letters," prepared by Professor Allen, gives many quotations from the notes of Mr. Brooks that show how systematic he was in his sermon preparation.

This "skeleton" should be written out in such a way that if a man should find it and nothing more he would have a fair knowledge of the line of thought the sermon followed and the content of it. "The sermon is a proposition developed, and a proposition is a sermon condensed."

For example, a sermon on Psalm 90: 1, "Lord, thou hast been our dwelling place in all generations," had this "skeleton." To have God for a dwelling place saves us, at first, from the sense of utter chaos in human history. Secondly, it saves us from the sense of unendurable chaos in the individual life. Thirdly, it saves our ethical life from weakness and degeneration. It gives moral backbone.

This outline crystallizes the whole sermon. It would guide a man's thoughts in meditating on the text, and it moves toward the higher interests of religious life.

Men differ about the prominence they will give to this " skeleton." Mr. Spurgeon used frequently to give it at the first of the sermon. For example, he, in preaching on Hebrews 12:24, said, " We have two things in the text. First, we have a comparison between the blood of sprinkling and the blood of Jesus; and, secondly, we have a certain condition mentioned." This concentrated attention on what he was saying in the first part, and created what the pedagogical writers call " expectant attention " for the second part.

At another time, speaking about the blood of Jesus, he pictures a sinner seeing it and he says, " The blood spoke to him of ' Love.' And the second thing it said was ' Mercy.' The third thing was ' Pardon.' The next thing was ' Acceptance.' The next was ' Adoption.' The next thing was ' Security ' and the last thing it whispered was ' Heaven.' " That order was itself attention-commanding, and led thought over the whole journey of a pilgrim—from the city of Destruction to Emmanuel's Palace. How incongruous and powerless it would be if the order of the parts were reversed so that the sermon begun with " heaven "!

South, the great English preacher, quite generally stated his line of thought at the first as a lawyer states his proposed line of argument. Oswald Dykes rather approves this.

Mr. Beecher did not do this. He said that it was not a good thing to throw away the power of curiosity. It was better to have both the anticipation of good things to come combined with the surprise when they did come.

But he always knew what his line of thought was and how he was to follow it. He knew what he was trying to do, and knew he meant to do it.

A series of sermons on connected topics is useful. A common purpose running through the series brings men to church with an interest preliminary to the sermon. Attention is thus both involuntary because of their general interest in the thread of the series, and voluntary because of their desire to hear your teaching about it. This expedient has great pedagogical value because it contributes to larger views of truth than the single sermon on a topic once in a while. This may require the advertisement of the topics in advance. But advertisement is not necessary except from Sunday to Sunday.

These suggestions by no means exhaust the expedients that are both effective and high-toned.

There is a caution to be exercised lest in the effort to gain and hold attention expedients be resorted to that take so strong a hold upon the attention that the purpose of the sermon is forgotten. The illustration, for example, may be such that it at once diverts the mind so thoroughly as to make it difficult to call it back. It becomes a dangerous rival of the topic of the sermon. It sets up in the mind a competitive establishment hard to deal with. This "playing to the galleries" is a political expedient for holding the evanescent attention of a crowd but it defeats the purpose of an educational discourse. Probably the striking phrases of Mr. Sunday, and to some extent those of his feeble imitators, stay in the mind longer and more vividly by far than the truths of religion they were intended to plant in the minds of the hearers. To the extent that such is the case they are a damage rather than a source of strength or usefulness and should be avoided.

Crowning all and infusing all with life and power is what we call " personality." That inner sense of being in the right, and a force of will that makes a man's voice thrill with a mysterious something, gather up all that I have mentioned and so unite them in a sort of personal appeal that on almost any religious topic, and to nearly every kind of a congregation, the preacher having it will gain and hold attention, and thus have the first requirement for teaching—educating, leading out, the hearts and wills of men to better things.

IV.

If the trumpet give an uncertain voice, who shall prepare himself for war? So also ye, unless ye utter by the tongue speech easy to be understood, how shall it be known what is spoken? for ye will be speaking into the air.— I COR. 14:8.

WORDS AS SYMBOLS

THE pedagogical principle concerning "symbols" Paul seems to have understood. Jesus also knew its value for it is said that the common people heard him gladly.

My own observation as I hear men preach, and as I read the printed sermons, confirms me in the belief that many of our ministers have not pondered deeply on the injunction that Paul gives us in the verse quoted above.

There is a reason for their delinquency very close at hand. They read books about religious things more than they talk with folks about them. They get a vocabulary from books, and they understand it, but their congregations, not being in the habit of reading such books, do not understand their words. For example, I suppose every studious minister knows what idea the word "functioning" is intended to convey. If he were to ask ten of the common men in the congrega-

45

tion what it means he would find nine of them
do not know.

I read this morning this sentence, "From a
cosmic point of view." I do not underestimate
the intelligence of the common man when I say
that nine out of ten will stop to think what that
word "cosmic" means, and then will not be certain about it. In both these cases the speaker
would, for nine-tenths of his audience, be "speaking into the air." In a somewhat lesser measure
the use of theological terms leaves the hearer, if
not in actual ignorance of the truth, at least with
confused, and perhaps erroneous ideas.

There is a responsibility upon all cultured men
and all educators to help the people to the use of
the riches of language. But as teachers of religious truth from the pulpit this responsibility
dwindles into almost no importance in the presence of the great desire of every good minister to
press home a truth of great value upon the minds
and the hearts of his congregation. We could not
forgive Paul if he had said, "I greatly desire to
make you Corinthians know Christ and him crucified, but I must first give you an example of fine
writing and an elegant diction." And it would
raise a great presumption against the genuineness
of a passage of the gospels if it read: "the learned
scribes heard Jesus gladly."

The man who desires to teach truth must give
great attention to the simplicity and clearness of

his language. I once gave an address to a company of young folks. It was on a somewhat technical theme. I tried to be clear. But I failed in some cases. As I went along the street after the address I overheard some one say to his companion, "I suppose that was a good address but it was too educated for me." If I had cherished any self-gratulation before, it was very decidedly checked by that remark. It will never do for the minister to have such comment made about his sermons by any considerable portion of his congregation.

But how shall we guard ourselves from the error?

Consider first the origin of language. There is great diversity of opinion among students of this subject.

The older view was that Adam was given a language full grown when he was created. Very little of that idea remains. Others think that language in its embryonic stage consists of some simple sounds by which the soul seeks to express its own emotions, as the crying of an infant. Men "shout for joy." We hear people singing at their work, when they are alone. It is an involuntary, solitary language of a heart full of contentment. It has no reference to other folks and no desire to communicate ideas. No opinion can be sustained which denies the fact of such soul language.

Another theory is that man was, and always has been, a social being. He never could be contented, like the eagle, to live by himself. He congregates. He is hungry for his kind. A woman was sent out from the city by some charitably inclined friends to have a home in the country. She had food and air and shelter. But she soon came back to the single room and the poor air and the scanty living. When asked why she left the paradise of the country and came back to the Gehenna of the city, she replied, " The air is good, and the food is good, but stumps are poor company." It has always been true that " stumps are poor company " for men and women. But company is not much company if there be no language in which to " swap ideas." So men having this hunger for mankind, and an intelligence suited to their situation, had furnished for them some language. It was primitive. It had few words. Its grammar was simple. With increasing experience, and with accumulated ideas it became richer and is still growing richer.*

The changes and additions result from new words and new senses of old words. The new words come from dialects of various places, from

---

* The English language, for example, shows that when, in 1846, Worcester made his dictionary, he added to former works 27,000 words. In 1857 he added 19,000 more, making 104,000 in all. Webster's dictionary of 1828 had had 70,000 words. His "Unabridged" of 1864 had 114,000. The "International" of 1900 has 400,000. The Century contains 450,000 words.

slang, from trade, and in greatly increased proportion from the scientific world. Every new invention demands a word to symbolize it.

The vocabulary of religious life has grown by the addition of those things which Jesus added to the thought of men. The Hebrew had his vocabulary. And it was rich. We find translations of it in the Psalms and the Prophets. When Jesus came, and the church was enriched by his teachings, religious experience became richer. There were no words to express it fully. Then the old Hebrew words were attached to new ideas. For example, " Church " was enlarged from the old conception; " sacrifice " became not so much a thing to make God favorable to us as to show our devotion to him; " kingdom of God " changed from a racial affair, having Jerusalem as a center and Jews as the blooded aristocracy, to a company of folks from every nation and tribe, but all recognizing God as King and Jesus as Leader and Friend; " forgiveness " took a broader meaning; " salvation " changed from a matter of outward conditions to an inward attitude toward God.

Then as the church grew and became an organized body it had its new terms. As theology developed it made its own nomenclature.

Thus the vocabulary of religious speech grew to its present size.

The function of words. It may be said of

nearly all words that they are arbitrary signs or symbols. Why or how they were chosen we do not know. They are here as signs only. Take the word " sin," for example. The eye sees a certain set of marks. We call them letters. That combination of marks we have been taught tells us that in reading it we are to make certain sounds. These marks might have been used to suggest different sounds.

Those sounds we associate with a certain idea. When a man says " sin " in the pulpit men associate with it certain notions of conduct that is below this standard. But his idea is the result of teaching. I once had a young woman of limited education come to me for examination preparatory to entrance to the church. I asked her if she had felt herself to be a " sinner." She replied with great indignation, " No, sir!" Seeing that she misunderstood me I said, " Do you never feel that you have done wrong?" " Oh, yes," she replied. " Very often." She had associated with the word " sinner " the wrongdoing that is ascribed to the woman of Luke 7: 37. Take the word " baptism." It consists of some marks of peculiar shape. They are the representatives of some other marks in the Greek language. What idea do these marks suggest? It is entirely dependent on what men have been taught to associate with them. A Baptist at once thinks of an immersion. Others think only of the ceremony connected with the consecration of an infant. The whole meaning of the word is dependent on the teaching that has been given, and the use with which the hearers are familiar.

So is it with all words. I, when a lad, used to hear the hymn, " I Love to *Steal* Awhile Away." I never could understand why any Christian should love to *steal* anything. And just what it was to steal " awhile " went beyond me. Another line was " spend the hours of setting day." That meant to me Sunday—the day in which we used to " set around "—as the poor grammar of our boyhood called it.

It is astonishing how many people have similar misconceptions of very common words. The words raise imaginations and suggest ideas of many different sorts. The terms " communion," " church," " hell," " inspiration," " infallibility," " soul," " spirit," " Pharisee," " hypocrite," and hundreds more are liable to be spoken by one man to convey certain ideas, but when they get to the other man's mind they are loaded with a very different sort of freight.

They may well claim the epithet that a prominent man applied to the words of his opponent: namely, " weasel words."

Great evils may come from this dubious and unenlightened understanding of words. Not long ago a prominent religious teacher wrote a paper on the " deification of Jesus." He meant by that word the process by which the disciples discovered the divinity of Jesus, and called him, therefore, " The Christ." But the audience—and they were ministers—and the editors whose fears were aroused, took the word to mean the ascription of divinity to Jesus which he did not deserve, as the Romans deified Nero. Some were really troubled to think that a good man was thus losing his Savior. And others—especially among those editors who think themselves appointed of God to flay the slightest departure of any man from the ideas which the editors inherited from childhood and have not since investigated—pilloried the writer in the weekly religious (?) press.

That man used the word in a correct sense. But it was not the common use of it. The unlearned misinterpreted it and did him injustice. At another time a man spoke of the Bible as " archaic." He used it correctly but in an unusual sense, meaning that it was ancient and hence needed interpretation into modern thought. His hearers understood him to mean that it was outgrown and worthless, hence to be laid upon the shelf. So another injustice was done.

These things show us that the minister has a double duty in this situation. He must find symbols that convey the ideas he wishes to put into the minds of his hearers. That is the first task he has on hand. He has a second and subsidiary task to enrich and correct the language of his hearers. How can he do this? *The first requirement is that we preachers have a clear idea ourselves.* That is, that we have an idea outside of and independent of any words we may commonly use to express it or convey it to others. Words are only the dress of ideas, and they should have more than one suit to wear. We may clothe them in another suit when we wish. Once secure a clear idea and we can make effective search for expressions. It will not do to be like the muddled preacher who said, " To make it clearer to you and to me, let us take an illustration." Clear thought must exist before it can be clearly uttered.

One of the best of practices is to paraphrase passages of scripture. That is, express the thought in your own language, using none of the words of the passage. If you can do this you may be sure you have the soul of its meaning. So also in seeking expression to an idea—especially a somewhat unusual one—try to tell it in several ways. If you can, think of it as it might be spoken to a cultured audience. And then think of it as it could be understood by the unlearned. It is said of Thorwaldsen, the great Norwegian sculptor, that he was at work on a statue of Jesus. One day he called in a child and asked her who it looked like. She told him it looked like some of the neighbors. He called her again after a few days and showed her the same with his modifications and with the same result. He was much discouraged, but worked on. After a time he called her again and this time she said, " Why that is Jesus." Then he knew he had succeeded. When a man has tried to express his idea until he finds the common man can understand it he is succeeding in some measure as the Savior did. The common people will hear him gladly.

The next important discipline is to learn the language of the people to whom we speak.

I have spoken about words being audible signs. If a man does not understand the signs he will be like a man trying to read messages written in cipher.

People have some language for religious ideals but it is limited and often peculiar. It is a dialect. The preacher must learn to speak it well. This can come only by conversation with people on the subject of religion. Many a man reads intelligently books about religion, but they are in the technical or the cultured language of the day. He tries to preach in that language and he is " a barbarian unto them," as Paul expressed it. In pastoral visitation, when it is really such, the conversation turns to religious things and that becomes a school of language for the minister. He finds how they struggle to express their experiences. Often they have found an expression of great force which tells the story beautifully.

Another source of help is the study of the

Psalms. They were the expression of experiences very much like those of this later day. So forceful and so appropriate were they that we find ourselves using the words for ourselves more often than the words of any other writings. How perfectly fitting are the words, " The Lord is my Shepherd, I shall not want." Or, " Jehovah is my rock and my refuge." " Out of the depths have I cried unto thee, O God." " Bless the Lord, O my soul, and forget not all his benefits." " I was shapen in iniquity." " O wretched man that I am who shall deliver me! "

People who read the Bible much always respond to the use of it in the sermon. It carries its own meaning to them easily.

Bunyan's " Pilgrim's Progress " is a valuable book in learning the expressions of the common people. It is true that some of the ideas that lie back of the allegory are now out of date, yet most of it is still suitable for us. We are still pilgrims seeking a better country even if we are not leaving a city of Destruction. We still have our difficulties though we are not so deep in the " slough of Despond " as Pilgrim. Doubting Castle is not in ruins yet. Interpreter still awaits the coming of the unlearned. Beulah sometimes cheers our weary hearts. The river of Jordan awaits us all. And it is to be hoped that, as we cross it, we shall have the help that Pilgrim had. To read the story gives us words and figures that are useful in formulating our own thoughts as well as helping us to teach others.

Some books of synonyms should be frequently consulted and words always used with fine discrimination. But at all costs of beauty, and all sacrifice of rhetoric, and all disregard of elegance, speak in a language that is " understanded of the people " as the prayer book puts it. Otherwise it will be " speaking into the air."

I do not forget that ministers have a duty to promote Culture. But it is subordinate to the duty of being understood. It is not necessary nor desirable to be coarse or uncouth. In my judgment the modern apostle of slang does not gain as much in making himself understood as he loses by the destruction of proper reverence. There are some things that are so refined in their nature that they lose by any coarse way of describing them. The packages in which fine goods are sent us enhances their beauty. The way a dinner is served gives flavor to food. The minister has a very useful opportunity to seek and impart expressions as beautiful as the ideas he expresses. By studied and frequent use he may lead his people into the possession of language itself harmonious with the best ideas.

It was said of a writer of poetry in England that " he just failed of being the *artist in words* that is able to make the same appeal in all ages." " An artist in words." That is an art worth

while. A member of the choir in a large Philadelphia church said to me about the pastor, " Oh,
he is an artist." The subjects about which the
preacher speaks are worthy the best of literary art
subordinate to utility. Or rather the finest art is
to make art useful. This speech will be " like
apples of gold in pictures of silver."

V

I have spoken unto the prophets and I have multiplied visions and by the ministry of the prophets have I used similitudes.—HOSEA 12:10.

METAPHORS AND SIMILES

IN the preceding chapter we have considered the importance and character of words as symbols of ideas: and noticed how it is essential to good teaching that the words be understood by the hearers. Following upon that we naturally come to the use of words to suggest ideas that they do not in their first and ordinary sense actually represent. When thus employed they are said to have a figurative use. And the figures are chiefly Metaphors and Similes. The Metaphor is a word used to convey an idea through a second-hand process. There is no good word to convey the idea directly. E.g., Jesus had an idea about the relation of his disciples to the world. He expected that they would make the community in which they lived pleasanter to live in, and would keep it from drifting into immoral conditions. In looking around for something to represent his idea he thought of salt. He knew that salt makes food pleasant to the taste, and keeps food from spoiling; so he said, "Ye are the salt of the earth." That was the symbol that represents their duty and influence in the world. The salt itself is the "basis" of the metaphor. The "point of likeness" is its savoring and preserving power.

He speaks about the salt, but he is thinking about his disciples. He calls them the "salt," and talks as if they were "salt."

Uses of metaphors. Metaphors have several lines of usefulness. *They convey ideas otherwise difficult to express.* No one fails to know what was meant when Jesus said, "Ye are the light of the world." It might not be easy for all to tell what they understand by it, but they know. The idea is conveyed swiftly and accurately. I have heard some very odd metaphors which, though not elegant, accomplished their mission. The colored woman wanted some soda water. She called for "that water that tastes like your foot's asleep." The deacon who was pleased with a candidate for the pastorate said to me, "Mr. S—— is the man who struck oil with me." A homespun man of noble spirit and easy manner in prayer prayed for the ministers: "O Lord bless them today. Teach them how to do the trick." Paul said, "We do not handle words of God 'with sleight of hand.'" Job said, "I am escaped by the skin of my teeth." But metaphors need not be thus semi-comic or grotesque; they may be elegant and grand. "The

Lord is my Shepherd." "The Lord is my light and my salvation." "Be thou my rock for a house of defence to save me." "Let them be chaff before the wind." "Thou hast been our dwelling place in all generations." "I will say of the Lord, he is my refuge and my fortress." Each one of these conveys an idea about God which like the brush lines in a portrait adds something to the expression—the mental picture of God. Without these we could not convey our thoughts.

They enliven the sermon. Monotony in tone puts folks to sleep; and sameness of phrase does the same thing. Metaphors are like changing tones in conversation that vary with the sentiment of the speaker as the ripples on the lake change with the changing breezes. Each one calls for a kind of alertness of mind, a grasping for the idea, and a kind of satisfaction at having caught it. This is the charm of literature. And there is room for the literary gift to use itself in the sermon. Indeed the literary element in sermons, while it must be simpler, and more modest than in books, is nevertheless like the seasoning of food. It gratifies the appetite and helps the mental digestion. It is worth while to study—to angle—for good metaphors.

They fix ideas in memory. One must use his imagination in listening to the man who speaks in metaphors and this use is what helps us to remember. The mind acts in two ways, and is therefore more active and hence has more records of what is said. No man having read the story of the Prodigal Son in Luke 15 forgot it.

They furnish completeness by variety of expression. They are like the different views of friends that are given us in photographs. Combined they make complete pictures. Thus in seeking to convey the idea of the completeness of satisfaction that Christ furnishes for the soul of man and the welfare of society. " Jesus is the lamb of God, the great high priest, the image of God, the Elder brother, the fullness of God bodily, the Head of the church, the all in all for humanity."

Speaking of the Bible, Dr. Ferris of Philadelphia said, " It has been the slave's book. It has been the poet's book. It has been the child's book. It has been the creator of countless Good Samaritans. It has been the hope and guide of the reformer. It has done more by the words ' Father, forgive them ' to breathe peace into the jangling and warring forces of human ambition and strife than all the systems of philosophy. Not until the human heart no longer aches with sorrow: not until the time comes when there remains no more a prodigal to be brought back to the Father's house; not until the time comes when the despairing and desolate call no more for help; until tears cease to flow, until love has no task to perform, until the cup of cold water is no longer needed to refresh the parched wanderer on the highway of life,—not until then will the Bible lose its power and beauty, and cease to be enthroned in the heart of our humanity." These repetitions add greatly to the effectiveness of the already beautiful descriptions of value to the Book of books.

Similes. Very much less imaginative, but more easy to grasp the meaning of, are Similes. They are comparisons expressed by the word " like," or, " as "—" the kingdom of heaven is like leaven." " As cold water to a thirsty soul, so is good news from a far country." " As the door turneth upon his hinges so doth the slothful upon his bed." " As a madman who casteth firebrands, arrows, and death, so is the man that deceiveth his neighbor and saith, Am I not in sport?" The book of Proverbs is a mine of such figures. These, like the metaphors, furnish countless expressions with which to convey the myriad shades of truth. They turn the whole world about us into a word-factory, an armory, a thesaurus, a living list of analogies ready for use in teaching truth, in conveying ideas from preacher to congregation, from teacher to pupil, in revealing the beauty of the Gospel.

One important rule is that such terms be used as the hearers are familiar with. To say that the pastor is the " fugleman " of the church, or the teacher the " fugleman " of the class, means nothing to those who are ignorant of the word's meaning. To say that the teachings of Paul are like the poems of Robert Browning is obscure and useless to all but thoughtful students of that writer's works. Similes from history are, to the non-reading part of the congregation, without value unless they are given with sufficient fullness to be self-interpreting. Dr. Jowett has an instructive, exemplary, and suggestive passage, " Can our language easily say all we have got to say, or does it fail to carry the glory we would fain express. Is it not true that our language is often too big for our thought, and our thought like a spoonful of sad wine rattling about in a very ornate and distinguished bottle. . . . When Paul, in Romans 12, begins to be hortatory, preceptive, practical, it is because he has already prepared the rich bed in which these strong and winsome graces may be grown. Every precept in the twelfth chapter sends its roots down through all the previous chapters, through the rich fat soil of sanctification and justification and the mysterious agency of redeeming grace." This passage exemplifies two of the strong qualities of Dr. Jowett's preaching—namely, his easy familiar metaphors, and his three and four fold repetitions of his thought under differing metaphors. They are like the blows of the hammer, one after another, until the nail is in and the head set.

To do this well requires thought and the exer-

cise of the imagination. One must learn to
" see " the relations of life and the functions that
material things perform. Then he will find material always at hand. An earnest purpose, un-
selfish, and,—except to be an effective preacher,—
without ambitions, will be to his powers of mind
and heart like the sun upon the fields,—it quickens
all and makes all fruitful.

VI.

Without a parable spake he not unto them.—
MATT. 13:14.

ILLUSTRATION

THERE are some essential parts of the Christian truth that we are commissioned to teach which are very difficult to impart by use of words only. With our best efforts, and with the most carefully chosen phrases, people see the truths like those who look at mountains through the smoky atmosphere of an August day. Nothing is clear. The truth about forgiveness—how shall we make an audience "see" it with the mind's eye? Or the truth about the grace of God—by what words alone can we make it anything more than an abstract, and hence an indefinite, thing for most people? The truth about the strange work of the spirit of God in human hearts—what vocabulary is sufficient to convey the meaning of it? These and other truths that are fundamental in Christian truth are never lit up by the sun of clear apprehension when we only use words.

But we are not left powerless before our task as teachers. We have what is commonly called "power of illustration," upon which we can depend for the most difficult problems in the impartation of truth. This power is at the first an act of our own imagination and second an appeal to the imaginations of the hearers. Professor John Tyndall, the great English scientist, used to say to his hearers when he lectured upon physical sciences, " I must ask you to try and visualize the invisible." Something of that sort is the purpose of illustration. To visualize the invisible helps us.

But the subject that is commonly called the " power of illustration " is almost necessarily divided into two sections. These appear at first much alike, but closer examination shows that they are quite dissimilar. We may call the parts Illustration and Exemplification.

Illustration proper, as the word signifies, is a means of throwing light on a subject. It has its real basis in analogy. It compares things in one sphere of thought with things in another sphere. It differs from simple comparison in that particular. Comparison puts one thing alongside another of the same class, but illustration puts one thing of one sort alongside a thing of another sort, but these have one or two points in common. Thus parables are illustrations. They have been called earthly stories with heavenly meanings. For example, consider the parable of the bad steward. There the conduct of the steward in his relation to his master is called wise conduct only in this one particular: he made use of his present oppor-

ILLUSTRATION 67

tunity to provide for future needs. There are
other points of interest but they are all left out
of account. He was dishonest. He was negli-
gent. He deserved some sort of punishment.
But none of these points were used. What the
Savior was seeking to teach was that men should
take the future into account. He wanted to make
the wisdom of that very evident. And so he
throws light on the matter by giving this story.
He made his point so plain that no thoughtful one
need misunderstand him.

Or take another passage. Jesus wanted to impress upon his readers the two ideas that are
central in the Gospel, namely, that salvation is
offered to all, but on condition of their faith. He
could say it, and he did say it, in various ways.
But to make it more clear he took a story from
the Old Testament with which his readers were
very familiar: "As Moses lifted up the serpent
in the wilderness even so must the Son of man
be lifted up that whosoever believeth on him shall
not perish." The only point of importance was
the lifting up into sight. That was used to show
that as the serpent was lifted up to men's eyes, so
Jesus must be lifted up to the view of men's
minds. And as all who believed God enough to
accept his way of deliverance from the bites of
the serpents were delivered from them, so all who
have been made to know of the Son of man and
who will accept him as God's way of life will

surely find it. If we read this illustration in connection with the story as told in the Old Testament the thought of the Savior cannot fail to reach our minds.

In using illustration it is very important that the point of comparison is made clear and prominent; otherwise minor things in the illustration will steal away the minds of the hearers.

Illustrations also have great value in awakening other activities of the soul than intellectual ones. Knowledge reaches the mind through the senses. Men hear, see, and then think. But there is a kind of knowledge that comes from the emotions, and from the sensibilities. When truth comes in at more than one window of the soul, knowledge is made clearer. Illustrations open windows. They stir emotions. They fix attention. The story of the Prodigal Son at once sets several sets of function at work. We are interested to know what came to the young man. Curiosity awakens. The imagination is awake as it seeks to picture the conditions of the young wanderer. We feel sorrow at his misfortune and pity for his hunger. Then a new gleam of hope for him as we hear him say, " I will arise and go to my father." Solicitous expectation arises as we see him approach the old home; then a great gladness as we see the father come out to greet him with tokens of glad forgiveness. All that sets the whole choir of the soul a-singing. The whole orchestra

ILLUSTRATION 69

of sympathetic gladness unites to fill the measure of joy that comes to us. And then the mind begins to think out the lesson of it all—God's readiness to forgive the repentant sinner. Thus by a dozen sources the truth about God comes into the soul; a dozen of its activities are set in motion. This permanently fastens the truth in mind.

Illustration is valuable in arresting the minds of hearers. It is not easy for an audience to hold attention to one monotonous line of thought any more than it is pleasurable to hear men speak in monotony of voice. The illustration varies the action of the mind, and enlists the whole set of its functions one at a time.

Illustrations should be from familiar things. The guiding principle in their use is that which directs all pedagogy, namely, " from the known to the unknown." If we take an illustration from things unfamiliar we only confuse the minds. The danger in using facts from the physical science is that the facts are unfamiliar. The minister who is reading as he ought will have many such within his reach but his audience is not acquainted with them. If he will use such it is necessary to explain the illustration so that its point is clearly seen. For example, if one uses the habit of some animal as an illustration of parental care and affection it will be necessary to state the habit of the animal if it is not a familiar one. If the illustration is from the habit of electricity it will be necessary to show the habit to those who are unfamiliar with that strange force. If it be from some Bible record it may be best to relate the instance for the sake of some who have not recently read it.

A recent writer says of modern religion, " It is appearing simultaneously around and about the world exactly as a crystallizing substance appears here and there in supersaturated solution." To the primary student of chemistry that is a very apt illustration, but to the uninformed it is meaningless.

The associations of an illustration are very important. Every story has its environment of association. And the environment may be the most effective part of the illustration. When President E. G. Robinson was pastor of a church in Cincinnati, Ohio, the question of slavery was a living issue. The church had a resolution that it should not be discussed in that pulpit for it created division among the members. Dr. Robinson was an enemy to slavery, and it was not easy for him to be muzzled. But he was also a prudent man and did not think best, by being rash in his dealings, to deprive himself of an opportunity to influence the public mind. He, therefore, adopted the policy that when he wanted an illustration showing any of the Christian graces in full measure he would take the case of some negro, some deeply pious slave. In that way he

ILLUSTRATION 71

would create both a sympathy with the negro and at the same time show that God is no respecter of persons but gives his grace richly to all that believe in him without regard to their condition of servitude.

This power of association is a subtle and swift agency. A minister once used as an illustration something about a horse in the stable. One of his thoughtful men said to him the next day, " Pastor, your story was a good one but it took us out of church to the barn and that was not a good thing to do."

If we should at this time use the Kaiser as an illustration of any virtue, the associations of barbarous cruelty and deepest-dyed savagery that go with his name would neutralize the illustration though it might in itself be perfectly just and correct.

Saloon-keepers may have qualities that are good, but to use them as illustrations would be futile because of the unmitigated wickedness of their business. The associations are all so bad that no amount of good in them personally can sweeten the atmosphere that surrounds the thought of them. Barrels of skunk cannot be sweetened by vials of cologne.

Mr. Beecher once used as an illustration of the reaction of selfishness in Wall Street the habits of a drove of hogs in the western farms. He pictured them as huddling together in cold weather to keep warm. The big ones in the middle and the little ones in the cold outside circle. Sometimes, he said, the pressure for the middle becomes so great that the big ones in the middle are crowded up on top of others and are thus set forth a prey for cold winds from every quarter. So he said the big dealers who are in the ring may get where all the greed of the Street converges upon them. This illustration, while it was perfectly fitted to show the one idea of the reaction of selfishness, carried with it such an association of these big dealers with hogs that the stigma has not left my mind in all these many years since he used it.

Illustration must not be taken for argument. This is a common danger to those easily given to illustration. It must be remembered that reasoning from analogy rests upon the fact that the things in the analogy are of the same class. It cannot be argued that human mothers will forget their offspring because birds and cattle do.

Nor may we say that because cattle are polygamous therefore humans should be. There is a great difference between the logical and the analogical.

Exemplification. The other part of what is called "illustration" rests on a basis quite different from that of illustration as we have been considering it. There is no analogy here. The imagination is not so fully awake as in the other.

ILLUSTRATION 73

It is rather based on comparison and induction. As comparison it puts a single case up to view as a sample of others. Suppose, for example, we wish to show what faith is. It is almost impossible to make the idea clear without examples. The scripture says faith is " believing that God is and that he is the rewarder of those that diligently seek him." But immediately the writer begins a long list of examples of faith to show more fully what he means. He cites Abel and Enoch and Noah and Abraham and Isaac and Jacob and many others.

Suppose we desire to define forgiveness. How difficult it is! We say it is the " restoration of relations that have been broken by wrongdoing." But that is very abstract. One could say that many times and leave his audience in the fog. But when we say it is that which took place when Jesus spoke peace to the woman who was a sinner; or when Peter met his Savior after the denial; or when Paul was made an apostle of the gospel he had sought to smother, these give a definition that is unmistakable, and at the same time kindles a desire to have the experiences which are used to show it.

It thus becomes a persuasive as well as an example. Suppose we wish to show the action of God's spirit in the human heart. What shall we say? What phrase is able to describe so subtle an operation? We may talk about " regeneration" or the "new birth" or the "birth from above." But how elusive is the idea! But suppose we relate the case of a man who was hostile to religious people and to religious conversation and to all religious meetings. By some mighty agency he becomes a regular attendant of the church, a student of the scriptures, a man of glad testimony at proper times concerning the grace of God. That makes the idea concrete and therefore reaches the minds of the congregation. All the more if the case is one of which they have some personal knowledge.

Suppose we wish to show the wide activity of the grace of God, and we tell of the woman in a heathen country who in the natural hunger of her heart for God bows before her idol, and with plaintive soul pours out her longing for divine help or comfort. The soul of every one who hears will feel, in spite of some theological dogma to the contrary, that God is not wholly indifferent to such of his creatures.

If we desire to tell something about "inspiration," we can tell how the desire to tell the good news of Christ pressed itself upon Judson until it took him to India. Or we may tell how the strange something kept working in our own hearts until we

"Came to Jesus as we were,
    Weary and lone and sad.
We found in him a resting place,
    And he has made us glad."

ILLUSTRATION 75

We may say that every grace and every virtue that is worth seeking has examples to commend it to us all.

This use of examples has also the very soul of the scientific method. It calls to the witness stand, as it were, the record of single cases and from these makes the verdict. It is induction from facts; it reasons from the particular to general principles. Thus it combines the value of the illustration with the value of evidence. It both convinces and encourages, or rebukes, as the case may be.

But here also we must be careful. *No induction is safe unless in the points involved in the argument the circumstances are alike.*

If two men are in like circumstances we may infer that what one will do the other will do. Since Jacob and ourselves are in very different circumstances we may not infer that because Jacob dickered with God and promised him a tenth, therefore the Christian should give a tenth to missions. The circumstances are so different that no inference of that kind can be made. But we may say that since Jacob was a man of religious mind he desired to make some return to God for his blessings, therefore we may expect that all religiously minded men will have a similar desire.

Because the Lord's Supper was first observed in the night does not teach that it ought always to be so observed. The common thing is that it be observed and its symbolism be understood.

Baptism was first given in the river Jordan, but we may not infer that all baptisms must be in the Jordan or any other river. But since it was given to all believers upon their confession of faith in Jesus we may infer that it is obligatory on all such now.

Because churches did not in the New Testament times have settled pastors we may not infer that they should not have them now.

And, coming out from the New Testament, we may not infer that because there have been great revivals in which many were brought to see Jesus the Savior with great mental struggle, therefore all men must have such struggles. We must know that the mental conditions are the same before we can make any inference on that point.

These are sufficient to show that Exemplification properly used is a great aid to the teacher in making plain and impressive the truths of the religion we try to teach. But it should be used with care and discrimination.

Before leaving this subject it will be helpful to some who think they have not the aptitude for illustration to say that the root of it is in all people. And it can be remarkably developed by care. I know of several men who had as they thought a very deficient power of that kind. They were

ILLUSTRATION 77

mathematical in their mental make-up. But by patient endeavor they became exceptionally good in this matter. And the very logical, mathematical turn of mind which made them doubtful of their own power as illustrators did, under the training, make them free from the dangers of becoming mere story-tellers. They became most interesting, teaching preachers. Their illustrations, instead of confusing and confounding, elucidated and edified.

VII.

REASONING

I HAVE said in a previous discussion that logic is not a set of rules for thinking imposed upon people, but is a statement of the way that all people do think. It is a chart of the road by which the mind travels from uncertainty to certainty about any subject of thought. It is a map that shows the way to some fountain of truth as it was learned by some one who found the spring and blazed the trail so that others may find it. It is useful for those who seek the spring, but are not able for themselves to find it.

Logic does not invent any truth, it only uncovers it. It is by some asserted that Logic does not add to our knowledge at all, but only adds to our certainty. But with the speculations of logicians we are not now concerned. Our desire is only to make use of so much of the subject as will help us to be more effective educators in religious matters.

Reasoning may, for our purposes, be classified as Deductive, Inductive, Analogical, and Intuitive.

Deductive reasoning makes simple propositions that express single truths, and by comparison of one proposition with others makes evident the truth of other propositions. For example, to use the old formula, All men are mortal; John Smith is a man; therefore he is mortal. Or this, All inspired scripture is profitable; this book is a part of scripture; therefore it is profitable. Or, God cannot lie; God said the soul that sinneth shall die; therefore the sinner will die.

Sometimes a series of propositions is used as, for example, Paul in his letter to the Romans, 10:13, says, " Whoever calls on the Lord shall be saved." How can they call on him of whom they have not heard? How can they hear without a preacher? How can they preach unless they are sent? Each step in that series presents a truth that is evident to the reader,—self-evident we may say,—and each one is a stepping-stone to the next. So the mind climbs up that stairway to its concluding statement that in order for all to have the great promise of salvation preachers must be sent to them with the message.

Or take the letter to Romans. In the first two chapters he shows by various witnesses, whose testimony the Jewish readers would not deny, that all men come short of the things that God desires for them. That every one fails to fulfil the law, and of course all are condemned by the law. But men do not want to be under condemnation of God's law. How can they escape if they are under the law? Then he goes on to say: But there is a righteousness of another kind even the righteousness that is by faith in Jesus. (Rom. 3:21.)

In our preaching there are some truths that will be made clear and emphatic if we use this formal way of presenting them. If it is well done it interests common hearers. It is not as dry as it is commonly supposed to be. It is at least a framework for our buildings. But for the most part the frame will need to be well covered to make it acceptable.

Inductive reasoning is examining a series of individual cases, and from their testimony inferring a general principle for guidance in life. This is the so-called "scientific" way. But it has always been the way of the thoughtful. When the Psalmist wrote, "Walk about Zion and go round about her. . . . Mark well her bulwarks, consider the palaces, that ye may tell it to the generation following," he used the inductive process. He examined the various defences—her towers, her bulwarks, her palaces, and from these concluded that she was strong and prosperous and able to continue. When the Syrian rab-shakeh

called to the Jews in Jerusalem (II Kings 18: 33),
" Hath any of the gods of the nations ever delivered his land out of the hand of the king of
Assyria? Where are the gods of Hamath and
of Arpad? Where are the gods of Sepharvaim,
Hena, and Iva? Have they delivered Samaria out
of my hand?" he was invoking the inductive way
of reasoning. When Gamaliel spoke in the Coun-
cil as recorded in Acts 5: 33-39, he reasoned in-
ductively.

This is the method when we summon various
witnesses to confirm the statements we are led to
make about the Christian life and faith. It has
great effect on really inquiring minds. It piles up
testimony. It accumulates force as it goes on. It
raises a probability and then confirms it by repeated instances. For example, see the second
chapter of Hebrews.

Analogical reasoning. In this, truth is only
partly expressed. If, for example, one says,
Abraham did so and so, the unexpressed idea is,
Then we ought to do so. Your heavenly Father
sends the rain without partiality; therefore we
ought to be impartial in our interest in our fellow
men. Gabriel did not bring railing accusations
against Satan; therefore we ought to be restrained
in our speech even against wicked persons.

This analogical process underlies the allegorical
interpretation of scripture—a system that has
more things to condemn it and more to sustain

it than can easily be enumerated. The basis of it is the belief that events in the Israelite history and great persons of the Jewish race were intentionally set forth by divine purpose to teach spiritual truth by analogy. It is so full of uncertainties, and so susceptible to misapplication, that no careful preacher will attempt to build any doctrine upon it. It answers very well to illustrate with, but as argument it is almost always weak. But there is a limited field in which it has value. For example, if the Israelites got safely across the Red Sea, yet because of their sins did not get into Canaan, it may be safely inferred that men who begin the Christian life and then fall back into sinfulness will not reach the kingdom of heaven. Or, if an earthly owner will take away the vineyard from the servants who fail to return its fruits to him, we may infer that God will take away from unfaithful churches their opportunities and privileges.

Men with good imagination development make a large use of this kind of reasoning.

Intuitive reasoning (so called for want of a better term). That is, it comes to conclusions without any conscious process of thought. It is swift and pretty sure. A closer examination of it shows that there is a process, however, but it is subtle. Almost any sermon of Jesus is a good example of this method. It is like this: Some generally accepted truth or some intuitive moral principle is quietly assumed. It is not mentioned, but the conclusions are based upon it and intuitively felt to be true. For example, Jesus said: If an earthly father will not give his son a stone when he asks for bread, will God do less when his children ask him? The answer is of course he will not do less. That assumes that men are made in the image of God and that goodness is the same in God that it is in men.

In the Beatitudes Jesus said, "Blessed are the poor in spirit for theirs is the kingdom of heaven." We ask why are they blessed? and the answer is, the kingdom of heaven in the Old Testament is said to be one in which all those who enter it will be happy in all things. That teaching all Jews believed. It was assumed to be accepted by all his hearers. And when he said the poor in spirit would enter it, it was evident they are blessed. So in all his teaching there is this undercurrent of assumed ideas and beliefs to which Jesus appeals without notice as the basis of his arguments and exhortations.

The logic of exhortation. It is common to speak of exhortation as if it were of less logical import than other forms of address. The exhorter in the Methodist church, for example, is regarded as a man of less mental training than the ordained preacher. But I think that is an erroneous idea. Paul did not exhort by teasing men to be good. It is not real exhortation to plead with men on the emotional side mainly. Those who fall into any line of conduct under the appeals to mere emotion will not stay in line. There are many men who have the gift of oratory and emotional influence. It is a mysterious gift of great value. But unless it is mingled well with the logical gift its results will be like morning dew in June. It will be gone—evaporated by noon. It was said by a man who heard the great oration about the " cross of gold " that he believed the orator—*until he got home,* and then he was ashamed of himself. I know of a minister who has some of the most ill-founded doctrines. He has a large congregation of white-headed saints. One of his parishioners in a former church went to hear him in a new field. His friend asked him if he could believe what that man preached. He replied, *" I do while I am hearing it."* To educate a congregation requires that men should believe what is taught *after they get done hearing it.* It must have the allegiance of their quiet judgment in their quiet hours. To exhort men in an effective way is to give them truth convincing to the minds, but after that, or during it, make the appeal that is filled with sincere desire for their welfare. Paul's exhortations are at the end of his letters. He begins with argument usually, and then come the appeals: " I beseech you, therefore, by the mercies of God," is his formula.

The logical discipline. In order to use the processes of logic it will be necessary that we have the processes so familiar that we, as a sort of second nature, think and speak in a logical way. One feels as he reads the Pauline letters that Paul was thus familiar.

And in order to gain that kind of familiarity it will be necessary to study the rules of Logic. Many of the readers of this chapter have long since—it may be—laid their text book on the upper back shelf of the library. It will pay well to clean it from the dust of years and read it again.

One must think clearly himself. This means careful scrutiny of one's own thoughts. He must know the exact process by which he came to his conclusions. He must know the real reasons that control his actions. Many times he will discover that the real reason is not the one he at first would give nor the one he is actually controlled by. It will lead him to open his own processes to the light of inspection. It may surprise him, but it will strengthen him.

Then when he has examined them he will need to test them. Let him take the place of a hearer who is critical and unwilling, and see if he can find a flaw in his own arguments. It has been said of the Swiss that they fight better on retreat than on advance. The Germans take much pains in preparing for what would happen if in any battle the enemy should drive back the front line. So it will be well to consider what will be the reply we make to one who finds a flaw in our reasons. We need to remember that a perfectly sound conclusion may be stated that does not at all come from the reasons given. For example, one might say we ought to believe the Old Testament because the Jews did. That has no force because the Jews might have been mistaken.

It might still be true that we are justified in believing the Old Testament record, and having confidence in its teachings. One might say we ought to keep the feet-washing ceremony in the church because Jesus gave it at the last supper. That conclusion may be wrong though the statement about Jesus is true.

It may be good and necessary to keep the Sabbath or a Sabbath, and yet that practice be not founded on the custom of the Jews in Jesus' time.

It may be true that, for a Jew, tithing was commanded. It may be true that one-tenth is the least that Christians should give to the work of the church. But it is not true that the Christian ought to give a tenth because the Lord required it of the Jews. The conclusion to give is, or may be, correct; but the argument is without value. It may be true that churches should have deacons. And it is true that the church at Jerusalem did have some men whom they called deacons. But it does not follow at all that because they had seven deacons every little church in the country must have seven, or that they have any. If deacons are needed we may of course have them and base the case on the need, not on the example of the church in Jerusalem.

Before presenting any argumentative discourses test the arguments with care, for if you appear to be incorrect in your processes it will lose you the confidence of the best men in your congregation.

A study of process. Another element in our preparation for argumentative discourse is a study of the processes by which others come to their conclusions. All men have reasons for their conduct. More often than otherwise they are not very clear in their own minds as to what those reasons are. It may need the expositions of the pulpit to discover to them their own minds. They need to be interpreted to themselves. Men say they stand by their church because they think it is right. It may be that it is because their fathers stood by it and family pride is the real reason. Men sometimes say they are desirous to unite all churches because they think that churches ought to be one. The real reason may be that they think others will come to them, or that it will be cheaper for them to maintain union churches than to have separate ones. Some man may hold to opinions with great tenacity because he thinks that if he does not the truth will suffer. One man becomes fairly hysterical because he hears that some one discredits the story of the virgin birth. He thinks the divine character of the Lord is in danger of being denied. If that be his fear it is important to show him that if Jesus was ever divine it was long before that birth. That was only the door by which a divine one came into human history. His argument is: Jesus is divine because he had no earthly father. To deny the virgin birth is to assert that he had an earthly father. Therefore to deny the virgin birth is to deny his divine character. If you could show him that his first premise is not true then his fears are gone. Many people think in this fashion: "True Christians do not often go wrong; I regret that I so often do so; therefore, I am not a Christian." If you can show them that a true Christian is one who is trying to follow Jesus though he often fails, his fears will vanish and he will become happy in his hopeful endeavors to improve. Many ministers in their desire to condemn wrongdoing say, "If a man does so and so he is not a Christian." That means to the common hearer that to be a Christian is to have attained already a very high grade of life. That is not the scripture idea at all. It reads, "The bruised reed he will not break nor the smoking flax he will not quench." Our Lord's teaching is that we need to become disciples and take our place among his scholars; and if we do that we shall not perish but shall have eternal life. In another place he said, "He that hath the Son hath life." It is already flowing through his soul.

It is a great but most useful study to find out the erroneous reason of people and correct their premises, thus securing a correction of their fundamental reasonings.

VIII.

*We speak that we do know, and testify that we
have seen.*—JOHN 3: 11.

We were eyewitnesses of his majesty.—
II PETER 1: 16.

THE POINT OF CONTACT

ONE of the great things insisted upon in all
works that deal with teaching is called "getting the point of contact." That is, finding something in the mind of the pupil in which he is interested that can be made a stepping-stone to the
thought that the teacher wishes to awaken in the
pupil's mind.

This requires some knowledge of the pupil's
interests, and some ability to couple it with the
lesson to be impressed. The study of the child
is therefore a preparatory stage in the process of
educating the child.

The same sort of necessity exists for the
preacher in his educational endeavors but it finds
expression in various ways. In writing about
"symbols" I have said that we must use those
the meaning of which is known. That is, in the
matter of words the "point of contact" is in
words that are familiar. Likewise an illustration

must be understood or the point of likeness must be made plain before applying it.

I want to speak now about the "point of contact" in larger matters. There must also be this contact in the ideas we seek to impress.

We must find a contact in thought foundations previously laid. No thoughts can be valuable which have no roots in past knowledge. Ideas, ideals, and resolutions grow out of things that preceded them. Rivers are the combination of little streamlets. If one were to seek the fountainhead of the Delaware River he would go up past Philadelphia, Trenton, Port Jervis, Walton, and Delhi, and out into the springs and marshes west of the Catskill Mountains. Christian faith is like the river. It starts in a thousand bits of inquiry, and many crumbs of information. The mind, acting under what is called "apperception," sorts, combines, absorbs, assimilates, until the Christian idea of life flows full and controlling. No "conversions" to Christian life are sudden. They may appear to the outsider as such. But the man himself knows that the impulses and resolutions date back. St. Paul stands out as the popular example of "sudden conversion." If his were such a case it is the only one given in the scriptures. And he said of himself that he was an extreme case, so that extreme sinners could find hope. All other cases are evidently the culmination of previous mental and moral experiences.

But even Paul was exceptional only in the intensity of his emotions, not in the vital elements of it. Long afterward he said that at the time he had what is called his " conversion " he heard a voice saying, " It is hard for thee to kick against the goads." But long before this crucial hour the foundation had been laid. He said in Philippians that he was of the best family stock among his people. He was among the best students in his theological class at the school of Gamaliel. He was so zealous for what he thought was right that he persecuted those whom he thought were wrong. In Romans he said that he fought evil in himself with great energy, but he found a law within him warning against the law of his mind that brought him into daily sense of being a captive. This acceptance of Jesus was then not a turning from irreligion to piety. It was only the sudden ripening of experiences long in the ripening.

To return then to the purpose of this chapter, we ask what is the relation of this to our preaching? Our answer is, *We must find in the lives of our hearers some real foundation and build upon that*. We must get down to some experimental things and in some way connect our ideas with them. As examples from the scripture, take the story of the first disciples as given in John. Andrew first findeth his own brother Simon and says, " We have found the Messiah." That could have had no meaning unless Simon had been before interested in the Messianic hope. They had both been looking for him. As soon as Andrew mentioned it, Simon was awakened with interest. It was the point of contact with him.

When Philip went after Nathanael he said, "We have found him of whom Moses in the law and the prophets wrote, Jesus of Nazareth, the Son of Joseph." Nathanael had evidently talked with Philip about that before. He was interested in the subject at once. That was their "point of contact."

When Paul spoke to the people of Antioch-in-Psidia he was a stranger to them. But there was a "point of contact" in the fact that they were in a synagogue. That meant that they were religious. And being in a Jewish synagogue it was evident that they were interested in the prophecies. So he began, "Men of Israel and ye that worship Jehovah," and then he went on outlining the history of Israel.

This same principle, which these men followed, though perhaps never having formulated it to themselves, must be our guiding principle. There is no use in wasting time on things that merely interest. It is not difficult to get attention to such things for a little. The important thing is to get attention to the kind of thing that can be made a stepping-stone to what we are trying to do. For example, it might be of interest if we were to speak of the history of some book of the Bible. In these days of inquiry this would have an interest for many. But if our purpose at that time was to advance men a little toward Christ Jesus that subject would not be a good stepping-stone for that object. Or suppose we were wishing to lead men to see their need of the Christian faith, it would not be helpful to tell them, " Paul says, all men are sinners." They would not accept that on his statement. No man can make another sensible of his sin by telling him he is a sinner. He will probably reply, " You are another." It angers men to tell them that. It may be ever so true, but they will not take it from you nor from me. We must find some other " point of contact." That is a point of antagonism and repulsion. We might say, " The best of us are sinners in that we fail to be all we desire to be. We often do what we know is not right. There is not a day with the best of us at whose close we do not have some note of disappointment about ourselves." That lays the foundation for the question, " What can we do about it? " It is a stepping-stone to what we are trying to impress.

Suppose we desire to give men a better confidence in the scriptures. It will do no good to insist that, " That all scripture is inspired of God and is therefore authoritative." In these days they will say, " How do you know it is inspired? " But we may call attention to some of our common experiences, and then show how they are beautifully expressed in the words of those who in the past had the same. We can show how the evil consequences of wrongdoing are portrayed in the Bible. We can refer to those who in great stress of heart have found faith in God as taught in scriptures a comfort and a stay. Thus they may come to feel that the scriptures tell the truth about our relations to God and our duty to men.

If men are in doubt whether the teaching of Jesus is true we may say to them as Jesus did to the same sort of men in his day, "If any man will do his will he shall know whether the doctrine comes from God." Ask them whether any teaching of Jesus which they have fairly tried has been a disappointment to them. The Psalmist learned that way a long time ago when he said, "O taste and see that the Lord is good; blessed is the man that trusteth in him."

The great problem of the preacher is, "How can I get the grappling hooks of my thought to take hold of theirs? How can I get down below the mere traditional beliefs which are already losing their hold upon men and get a foundation in experience?" Unless we can do that we shall have poor success in leading men to better things.

A genuine interest in men for their own sake is one line of influence, one "point of contact" which is always effective. Such an interest gives a tone and a potency to a speaker's words which is a meeting-place at once. Men all appreciate sympathy and are all interested in their own welfare. The man who evidently seeks that has a foundation upon which to build. The results are not always immediately apparent, but they are sure. Henry Ward Beecher in one of his lectures told of a man who, under the preaching of the elder Beecher, Henry's father, withstood all his appeals so far as making a public confession was concerned. But when Mr. Beecher moved to the West he left the grave of a little child alone in the East. This man took up the little body and made a grave for it between the lots he had provided for himself and his wife, saying that Mr. Beecher's child should not be left alone. That was the delayed result of a genuine influence of the preacher on that man. I take it that real sympathy is never wasted, never uneffective. It is always a meeting-place, always a " point of contact" from which real influence can proceed.

The " point of contact" must be that which is useful for the purpose of the particular sermon. What would be a good one for some sermons would fail in others. What is foundation for one kind of an address may not fit another. It would not have been effective if Paul when in Athens had begun by referring to Moses. They would have asked, " Who is Moses that we should hear him? "

There are introductory remarks that are useful

in conciliating a hostile audience. Such were Paul's remarks on the steps of the tower when he was arrested in Jerusalem. But these are not really foundations for teaching. The real point is something that can become a part of the building of thought we are seeking to have them construct so that what they are led to think will be an outgrowth of what they have experienced. More and more we are coming to see that the real faith of the Christian man is founded on experiences. No second-hand faith will satisfy us. And we are coming to see that no truth is valuable that cannot be transmuted into experience by adopting it heartily. Hopes for the future are really without solid underpinning unless they are built upon experiences in this world.

Doctrinal " points of contact." In a somewhat different field this principle is even more vital to a Christian life. There must needs be something in the nature of a " system of doctrine." Made up as we are, we need standards with which to compare our judgments in individual cases. In Ethics, for example, we instinctively decide each judgment by comparing our first impressions or our desires with our standard of right. So in thinking about religious truth we need what we may call a " standard of orthodoxy." This standard may be one of our own making, or it may be one that we have accepted from the church or from public opinion. No small part of the pastor's duty is to secure in the minds of his congregation a correct standard of truth. This is especially true in those churches like Baptist and Congregational where authoritative or ecclesiastical standards do not figure very largely but individual freedom is exercised. But no man has a real right to be inconsistent in his thinking. Nor has he a right to be erroneous in his opinions. And no pastor can be indifferent to the intellectual views of religious matters in his congregation. It becomes a part of his duty, therefore, to help in building up in the minds of his hearers a correct, consistent set of opinions on the fundamental principles of their faith.

What I wish to emphasize just now is this: All opinions and all doctrines to be valuable must rest on facts. They must be gained by an inductive study of experiences. The point of beginning in any system is in what some one experienced. The scripture is all of that sort. David experienced a great trust in God based upon his experience. He wrote out his feeling of trust in the Twenty-third Psalm. Peter experienced great change in his life by reason of his faith in Jesus. And he wrote because of it that, We are made partakers of the divine nature by great and precious promises. John wrote about the things we have seen and handled of the word of life. Paul began his new theology when he had a call from Jesus on the way to Damascus. From such facts in the writers' lives their doctrines were developed. Each year of life added something to the extent and the certainty of their faith.

The pastor, therefore, in his instruction must build on experience. To thunder out his own anathemas, or to quote to the modern man with pompous tone the words of creed or confession as if they were the bottom stones of all opinion is to waste time. Creeds may be used as confirmation of views tentatively gathered from experience. They combine a vast amount of experience from other lives. But as *authority* they are not acceptable. For a pastor to read men of any sort out of the kingdom of God and doom them all to hell as if he was a divinely appointed judge, as some of the modern evangelists do, is not only powerless to lead any one in the path of truth but is disgusting to all quietly thinking men.

To follow this principle will sift out much of so-called theology from the common mind. It will re-examine the premises, and soon mark with the brand of uncertainty some statements of wide circulation. For example, it is not uncommonly said that all men are hopeless sinners, having no power to choose good and little power to see it when it is before them. Therefore, it is of no use to urge men to accept a savior whom they cannot appreciate. That is a perfectly sound conclusion if *the premise is true*. But the premise is not true. Every man knows that he is not power-less. He does see and does reject. He might choose. No man as he looks back on any action but knows that he might have done the other thing. All theories of total depravity to the contrary he knows better than to say he could not have done otherwise. To build any set of ideas, therefore, on an assumed premise which experience and consciousness disputes is to build on the sand. No man condemns himself in any act without in that very condemnation admitting that he might have done the other thing. And no man can have any self-approval if he does not know that he chose the way he went for himself.

This starting in the facts is the point of contact with thinking men from which and upon which the doctrinal buildings can be satisfactorily established and permanently remain.

"Our fathers talked a great deal about 'experiencing religion.' The phrase has died out in our vocabulary. I wonder why. Can it be because religion has ceased to be an 'experience' to us, and has become a mere theory? Perhaps it is what Leslie Stephen so caustically calls a 'fine art.' What is Christianity? A song, whose rhythmic cadence soothes the imagination, and satisfies the esthetic sense! A picture, dramatic or pathetic, that leaves a lingering sentiment in the soul! A doctrine, to be studied and discussed and argued, until the mind grasps its significance! A dream of old Galilee, that tells of the glory and beauty of One who lived under Syrian skies! No, Christianity is more than these. It is a *life*." *

* George Hooper Ferris, Philadelphia.

IX.

Christ suffered for you, leaving you an example that ye should follow in his steps.—
I PETER 2:21.

IDEALS

THERE is a great difference between an ideal life and an ideal "in" life. That little word "in" changes the meaning of the sentence from a general standard of life to the very motive of life; from the goal toward which the runners are all to look as they run to the runner himself; from an idea of good health to the care with which we seek it. A man may have a very high ideal of life and be a very low man in life. He may have a deficient ideal and be very high in the quality of his life. With the Christian Jesus is the ideal man—the man we know we ought to be like. Our ideal is the man we really try to be like.

The ideal is the mainspring of life. Whether it be high or low it controls in the most subtle way the course we run and the way we run it. A minister reads about the kind of minister the writers think he ought to be and assents to it verbally. At the same time he tries to be some other sort of a preacher. He may imitate the

slang of a Billy Sunday or, swinging to the other
extreme, he may try to preach in the dignified
style of a Webster. This is, on the surface, a
mystery. We may see great icebergs moving
south in the Atlantic, going against wind and
Gulf Stream. It looks mysterious, almost un-
canny. But to the informed it is simple. Six-
sevenths of the bulk is under water. It reaches
down into the cold currents that run south toward
the equator and the bulk of its substance is controlled by that current. So men go with the
deepest current of their desires. While they are
evidently facing one way, in their hearts they
are going another way. Some went to California
in the gold times of '49 and became thugs.
Some go from the East where they have been
members of churches and forget the church and
join the world. When they were at home they
belonged to one denomination. After they got
away from the home influences they joined
another. It was in their hearts all the time. The
law of the ideal works as surely the other way.
Many a man has remained in bad company from
force of circumstances. When he could he broke
with them entirely. We remember how Vice-
President Arthur was called a political trimmer
who leaned toward all sorts of machine politics.
The whole nation was afraid of him when he
came by a stroke of a murderer to be President.
But the training of a godly father and mother

was the deepest current and he swung out into it when he could and won the respect of all. Mr. Cleveland was at one time anything but a man controlled by good ideals. But it came to pass that the deep current of a godly father's and mother's influence asserted itself, and he became an active member of the Christian church and was no dishonor to it. Many men have lived in poor houses because they had no better. But with prosperity they built homes of beauty. They had the desire all the time.

This mighty force determines the direction of men's courses. It measures their value. It determines their future destiny, for, as Jesus said, "Out of the heart are the issues of life." If we ministers can affect it we touch the helm of life.

It will be helpful for us to analyze this powerful element and find if we can the process of choosing the ideal.

Individuation. In the study of the psychology of youth we find a strong tendency amounting at times to a conscious and determined purpose to have an individual life. They want to sit by themselves in church; to choose their own company; to select their own amusements; in other words, they *"want to do as they are a mind to."* That same tendency, modified by experience, and by the demands of society, is the foundation of democracy in politics, of Protestantism in religion.

It has its great nourishment in the New Testament doctrine of an individual judgment. " Every one shall give account of himself to God "; and in the doctrine of Providence, " Not a sparrow falls to the ground without your Father." If men are sons of God who is commissioned to be their ruler? No preaching can be of influence if it ignores this tendency—this process of *individuation*. A further study of this tendency shows us that it is the determining factor in the choice of our ideals. We want to *" do as we are a mind to."* But what are *" we a mind to do "* and why are we " a mind to do so? " Jesus said to some Jewish people who did not accept him, " Ye will not come to me because ye are not of God." That is, there was a reason back of their rejection of him. It was their great unlikeness to God. So now there are great deep undercurrents of likes and dislikes that determine what we are " a mind to do." If we follow the stream back we come to some as yet unexplored wilderness where the stream of life has its beginnings. The " mind to do " is a complex affair. Family inheritance, environment, early training, later instruction, social demands, the Holy Spirit—each and all have a share in the work of creating the " mind to do."

But there is always a " mind to do " something, and that something is to attain our ideal in life.

Choice rests upon estimate of values. We make our choices in life by that which at the time we deem of most importance to us. We choose that which for us at the time is worth most or which will, we think, in the long run, be of most service. If a man thinks that money is of more value to him than good character he will choose as his ideal a man successful in getting wealth by any means. His motto will be, " Put money in thy purse."

If to him good character is of greatest value he will be sure to take a righteous man as his ideal. In all cases it is a question of valuation.

But why does he value one thing more than another? That question reaches toward depths greater than we can fathom. But we can sound a part of the depths. If a man or a child has found pleasure in any action it is the natural thing to want it again. If it gives repeated pleasure it becomes a constant object of pursuit. He chooses the course that will secure it. If a child never heard music he never would choose to be a musician. If he never had the pleasure of doing things he would not try to do them. If he never knew the comfort of forgiving he would not seek to have a forgiving spirit. If he does know the pleasure and the profit of being always truthful he will make truthfulness one part of his ideal in life. If he knows the pleasure of helping others he will put a wholesome altruism into his ideal. So, all the way through the list, experience in the pleasure or the profit of right actions or harm and discomfort from wrong actions determine the lines of the portrait they make for themselves of the men they will seek to be.

There follows from this that the parents are the first who have the opportunity and the power to give them a taste of what is good and a taste of what is bad. Thus the appetite so to speak will be formed and that appetite will later determine the choice of ideal.

A pious old minister with a keen insight was deeply concerned in the welfare of a fatherless grandson. He took him with him when visiting the poor of his parish in the valleys of the Alps. When they entered the poverty-stricken houses of the poor the boy said, "When I am a man I mean to take the side of the poor." That boy was Henry Pestalozzi, a father to orphans and the founder of universal elementary education. He tasted the joy of helping others.

The motive that underlies the efforts of parents to have their children give of their own little funds to mission work is to give them a taste of its joy, so that they will afterward choose to be generous. All the great features of a good ideal may thus, by wise parents, be in large measure predetermined.

The ideal changes with experience. A liking thus germinal in youth may become controlling in later years. The ideal may become more complete and decided as experience increases. If a man upon mature reflection decides that to be strictly honest is best for him he may come to see more clearly the excellency of his choice. He may be instructed by many agencies concerning the demands of honesty. Thus his ideal will become richer and more commanding. He will fight more earnestly against whatever may be contrary to it.

It may be that a man has deliberately chosen to be a mature Christian man. He has settled that primary element in his ideal. He may have said with a man of old, " As for me and my house we will serve the Lord." He does not know all that is implied in that decision but he has made it. Later years will make it more evident that he chose wisely. His ideal will remain but will grow into larger proportions and more beauty of holiness.

When are ideals formed? A large proportion of them are formed early in life. Two leading historians of America,—Prescott and Parkman,— made the choice of their life work as historians while in college. They followed the choice. It was their great contribution to the knowledge of the history of America's early days. Nearly all ministers have had the first movements of their heart's toward the ministry when they were in their teens. In the matter of the Christian life it not infrequently occurs that the true estimate of values is delayed to later years. By some mighty presentation of the character of Christian life men are—the spirit of God co-operating—made to see what they had not seen. Their estimate is changed and therefore their ideal changes. They adopt in later life what many others adopt earlier. But the process is the same.

From these considerations we see that the pastor can be of great service by presenting to the congregation the attractive side of the Christian life. All the ability we have can find use in this. To tell in words the excellence and the beauty of holiness is a task worthy our most careful study. Many of its beauties are unspeakable. But all may be made agreeable. It will be helpful if you often try to think out what are the excellencies and beauties of the Christian life. Try to see its beauty for yourselves. Then read the expressions that others have used to impart their conceptions of it. Afterward carefully seek words and illustration to convey your own thoughts about it. If the ancient preacher, " because he was wise still taught the people knowledge and sought to find out acceptable words " (Eccles. 12 : 9) when he had so meager a tale to tell of God's goodness, much more may we spare no pains to tell the goodness of God and the comfort of serving him in an attractive way.

I can but think that in our day there is more endeavor to scold people for their shortcomings than to win them by attractive presentation of the Christian life. The Psalmist wrote, " I will *bless the Lord* at all times; his *praise* shall continually be in my mouth. . . . O *magnify* the Lord with me and let us *exalt his name* together." (Ps. 34.) A young man of whom I knew, brought up in a good family and at heart disposed to be right, declined to go to church as he said " to be lectured to all the time." An old Christian once said to me, " Molasses catches more flies than vinegar." Men are not made better by scolding them. It is said by teachers that boys are sometimes made to dislike Arithmetic because their first lessons in it are made disagreeable by poor teaching. In times of great discouragement the minister needs to visit the throne of grace until he can see through the clouds and be *triumphant himself*. To be all the time telling people what they are not to do, and what things they do that are not right, makes the course of the Christian look forbidding to the young and the old. The " common people heard Jesus gladly." And it was because he told them that the poor in spirit would have the kingdom, and that God would accept the sinners who came to him, and that there would be plenty of harvest even if the birds and the tares destroyed some of the good seed, and the leaven would make the meal to be leavened in time, and said Come unto me and find rest unto your souls.

He went about all Galilee preaching the glad tidings—not the doleful ones—of the kingdom. I do not mean to suggest that there are no serious and sad and awe-inspiring things to be spoken, but the prevailing tone must be joyous and triumphant. Our weekly papers do us great harm by frequently printing the records of the incompetency of churches and their earth-mindedness. More often they tell about the failure of the churches, and the losing of power over the common people. All this is first erroneous. It is not true to the whole situation. And second it is poor policy to be telling all the world and all the young Christians the family frictions and personal weaknesses that are after all only specks on the picture.

Present the finer lines of a good ideal. Most people have a sort of charcoal sketch of what they want to be, but the details are not put in. To show them the application of Christian principles in the various circumstances of life is to show them the exceeding great value of the Christian religion. Their estimate will grow, and thus their devotion to the ideal will increase.

This is done mainly by the presentation of the lives of others who have taken the same ideal. In this the records of the Bible characters are rich in value. A pastorate that has made the congregation to be familiar with what underlies the

stories of Abraham and Moses, Samuel and Elisha,
of Ruth and Boaz, of Isaiah and Hezekiah in the
Old Testament; and of Matthew and John and
Peter among the Apostles of the New Testament,
has done a great work for the ideals of his people. But Christian biography is a continuation of
the list quite as rich and useful as the biblical list.
Piety did not die out when the last chapter of the
New Testament was finished. As good men live
now as then. And in their comprehension of the
Christian life those who live now have a much
broader and finer ideal than the Apostles themselves. Paul said, " I have only laid a foundation; others must build thereon." Others have
been building ever since. At times the work has
gone slowly; but this generation is far richer in
its ideals for society and far more efficient in the
earthly side of the kingdom than any one was in
Paul's time. They had the germinal idea. In
their day the blade, later the ear, and some time
the full corn in the ear will appear. Let me not
be understood to say that the ideals of the individual life were incorrect, or that they were not
fully in sympathy with the spirit of the kingdom.
They were. But they did not know, and could
not know, the sweep of the Christian gospel
through the world, nor the subtle power it would
have in leavening not only the church but the
whole world in which the church would live. The
light of the world it has been; the salt of the

earth it always will be. Christian biography, I repeat, is a mine of wealth for ideal-making material. And we include not only martyrs, who died for the truth, but men and women who lived for it; who put the best brains and the greatest wisdom into the work of preaching, teaching, organizing on large scale human activities for the good of men. The founders of charities, the establishers of hospitals, the investigators of science for the prevention of diseases, the consecration of wealth for the common good; the students of history to discover the best way to govern men; the musicians who have sought to uplift our hearts in great oratorios; the architects who have sung their "hymns to God in obedient stone"—all these are diamonds from the mines of history to enrich our ideal of life. Culture, broad and careful, finds its field of usefulness in this work of ideal making by showing the value of the Christian life to single souls and to society.

A neglected field of study for this work is the lives of women. Once a request was made of a large section of the public school teachers of New York City that they secure from their scholars the name of the person they would rather be if they were to be some one else than themselves. The reply was wide in its scope, but the astonishing thing was that not a scholar even among the girls expressed the desire to be like some woman.

The superintendents regarded that as a serious comment on the teachers. They had not taught their girls concerning the lives and characters of great women. It was not really a fair criticism, for the school books did not furnish such material. The biographies of noted women, especially of mothers who brought up families in the nurture and admonition of the Lord, ought to be a theme often treated in the pulpit and used in illustration. The young women need the material of that sort in the choosing of their own ideals. The Bible itself is not abundant in such material, but Ruth and Hannah and Jael and Elizabeth and Mary and Dorcas and Timothy's mother and grandmother and Priscilla and Lydia furnish suggestions for good thoughts about good women.

But our modern life is as full of noble women as the heavens are of stars. Let the records of missionaries and teachers and Red Cross leaders be consulted and there will be no dearth of material suitable to enthuse girls with noble ideals.

The pastor's largest opportunity is in presenting the value of the Christian life in its larger aspects. Paul wrote that he determined to know nothing but Christ and him crucified. That is very far from saying that he would know nothing but a crucified Christ. He would know *nothing but Christ.* What a knowledge that would be! He must tell men all that he could about him. He told of his resurrection, of his exaltation, of his kingship, of his sitting at God's right hand until he became conqueror, of his return to take his people, of his being judge of the quick and the dead. It is written in the gospel of John that as Moses lifted up the serpent in the wilderness, so the Son of man must be lifted up before the world. To preach and to teach about Christ so that one can have a definite idea of what he is to do, and how it is to be done—that gives a value to the Christian ideal which will lead men who are seeking goodly pearls to sell all they have and secure it. He will be to them the "chiefest among ten thousand and the one altogether lovely." They will "behold as in a glass the glory of the Lord," and thus be "changed into his image from glory to glory even as by the spirit of the Lord."

X.

If any one is a hearer of the word and not a doer he is like unto a man beholding his natural face in a mirror; for he beholdeth himself and goeth away, and straightway forgetteth what manner of man he is.—JAMES I :23.

SELF-ACTIVITY

AN indispensable result of all true educational processes is the exercise of the pupil's own powers. No one can become a musician by simply studying the theory of music. His own fingers must strike the keys of the piano; his arm draw the bow of the violin; his lips fit the mouthpiece of the cornet before the first elements of a musician can be found in him.

Books of physiology may be mastered, theories of gymnastic cultivation be understood, but no half inch of measurement to his muscles, and no half ounce of new strength to their power can be gained unless they are made to *act*. The boy must lift or he will never be strong; the runner must run, the thinker must think, the preacher must preach if there is to be any gain in their efficiency. So the educators must study the art of getting pupils to *act*. Self-activity is a " *sine qua non* "—a " without which nothing."

In the musical field it is not difficult to secure it. Every pupil expects to " practice " from one to five hours a day.

Athletic ambitions lead the boys to run and jump for prizes. If they work at muscular occupations they get the activity incidentally in their tasks.

But when the teacher is imparting ideas and cultivating character, the work of securing the exercise of whatever function the teacher desires to improve is complex.

For example, if a teacher is seeking to impress the value of honesty how, in a class, can he call out self-activity? If a minister is preaching about the virtue of forgiveness, how is he to induce men to forgive? If he wants them to have a high estimate of their church, he will need to make heavy drafts upon his reserves of ingenuity to find a way to do it.

But he will find some ways at hand if he remembers that some of the functions of mind and heart can be exercised very much by the imagination.

I once had a boy in my church who stabbed another boy without any great provocation. I went to see him to try to find out the secret cause of it. He told me that he was accustomed to read all the records of fights in the daily papers. He had been " putting himself in the place " of the criminals until he was like a good actor, possessed by the criminal of whom he read. Thus his mind had become trained to " think stab " and his hand almost practiced in the art of stabbing. Thus on the slightest provocation his " will to stab " went off like an explosive at the tiniest spark of fire.

If you study your own consciousness you will very probably find that in these times when you read the tales of war atrocities you are already half prepared to take vengeance on those who do them. One of the moral damages of war is this blunting of the soul to the influences of mercy and forgiveness. It is easy to explain. The will to do warlike things is half exercised in the imagination. All the feelings of revenge and hate are awakened and called out like scholars in a fire-drill, and thus become experts in getting ready for a real action.

This principle, so effective in evil, is our great ally in good. Self-activity can be very closely approached by the exercise of the imagination in the lines of action desired. Thus a preacher that much of the time presents the faults of people, their shortcomings, their inconsistencies, their semi-hypocrisies, their unsocial conduct, will produce a querulous, hypercritical condition in the congregation.

On the other hand, the sweet and sunny and hopeful preacher will have a congregation with whom it is pleasant and helpful to worship and work.

Coupled with this we must seek to *discover ways that will commit the people by* an *act* of *the will.* To be specific: suppose we are in an evangelistic meeting, or campaign, we need, in addition to awakening the desire to be a Christian, some *act* by which the will is committed. This is the value of the old-fashioned "mourners' bench," or the "stand up," or the "strike the trail" devices.

Many an evangelistic sermon has been successful in creating a readiness to accept the Savior, but the custom of the church does not provide for any action at the time, and so the man goes home and the impression cools off. He has heated the iron to workable heat and then plunged it into cold water and it is hardened. It will pay well to have some always-at-hand method of getting the will at work every Sunday, to secure action on the part of serious-minded people which will commit them to the Christian life. It may be an opportunity to meet the pastor, or to write their names in a book for that purpose, or to come forward at the close of the service—any way to conserve the impression the sermon has made and not send men home to forget it.

Suppose you have a missionary sermon. Of course, you are not satisfied to have the people know about missions. You seek to have them become partners in the great enterprise;—to "take some of the stock." Some provision must be made to " secure the money for the stock." I once was asked to preach a missionary sermon in a strange church. I did so, and it was said by some that the appeal was " very effective." But I learned that the church was under the law of a few men who said " we never take a collection." " Our people are all poor folks." And so a collection was not taken. That was not only waste of my time,—just burning powder in fireworks for display,—but it was hardening the hearts of the congregation. It accustomed them to emotion without action so that they would sleep under it as men who sleep on the cars get accustomed to noise. There should always be some sort of provision for the pledge or the actual contribution, or some identification in heart with a specific, concrete mission.

Suppose you are seeking to secure more faithful attendance at the church. You will of course try to show the advantages to be gained by it. But you will do the important thing if you say, " Now will you not promise yourself to come for the next four Sundays or Wednesday nights? "

But some one may say, " We do not always have these concrete things in mind; we are aiming at what we may call general spiritual culture. We are *instructing* in theology or in the graces of the Christian life."

It is true that such aims do not furnish ways for physical self-activity. But there are ways in abundance for the mental activities you seek to secure.

In the case of the reasoning faculties, all reasoning processes followed in your sermon call for the activity of their minds as they follow your thought. This is the great value in the skeleton of a sermon. It furnishes a track for the mind to follow. If a hearer is kept running around for your main purpose like a hound snuffing for the trail of a fox, not much educational good comes; but if there is a line of thought he will exercise his mind in following it.

Suppose you seek to develop the moral judgment. You can do it by stating problems. You may say, "In such and such a case, what is the right thing to do?" "Will a man under such and such conditions be justified in doing so and so?" "What will the effect be upon a man who does so and so?" "Mr. So-and-So did this or that, he was not popular. Why so?" "What are the ripened fruits of untruthfulness or hatred?" Thus you will lead them on to the right conclusion only after they have been thinking out for themselves the proper reply. To tell them dogmatically "this is wrong" is not as profitable as to ask them "is this right?" Such methods set the minds of the congregation at work. They do not open their mouths like young robins to be fed; they sally out under your guidance to find their own food and thus grow into maturity of thought. The question method is a very effective one for inducing self-activity of mind.

In the matter of church support, as I have suggested in the chapter on church management, it is important that the young be enrolled as contributors, thus giving them weekly action and weekly thought about the church.

If one seeks to develop the grace of forgiveness, the most that seems practicable is to present the duty of forgiveness; to portray and exemplify by illustration until it is made to appear desirable, and then suggest with great definiteness that if any feel estranged toward others they should at the earliest opportunity begin some *acts* of *kindness* toward them. Words of forgiveness are good, but acts are also good. Forgiveness means the restoration of broken relations. This is accomplished by *resuming the relations.* To stand off and be " willing to forgive " is no forgiveness at all. Horace Greeley used to say, " The way to resume is to resume "; and the way to resume kindly relations is to resume them.

Suppose you wish to increase the Bible-reading practice; then provide some plan to unite all in Bible-reading on some subject and have a meeting soon to hear what they have learned. A paper now and then by some one, read in the midweek meeting on a Bible character, or a Bible doctrine, enlists and interests the writer and the hearers. If you are wishing to have your people take more interest in community betterment, devise some work within their reach that they can *begin to do* and the taste for it will lead on to more skill, and better success and larger plans.

In these ways you will find your people will come into the habit of thinking in practical lines and you will be made glad to see that they are being truly educated in the Christian life.

XI.

The love of Christ constraineth us.—II COR. 5:14.

MOTIVES

I HAVE spoken in the former discussion about the forming of ideals and shown how they are chosen because of a liking for them. Then I pointed out that all learn to like good things by tasting of their results. This led us to the place where we are to ask how can we get people to try good things? How can we get them to what is called self-activity along these lines? This brings us to the subject of motives. That is, to the question, what means can we use, what springs of action can we touch, what influences can we bring to bear to get people into motion? The following is from a daily paper concerning Mr. Sunday's methods: "There can be no doubt that Mr. Sunday's methods, frequently attacked but almost invariably successful, are worked out to the last word or action, and that they have been *reduced to a science long ago*. He leads up to a climax with a series of 'hell-roaring cries,' as he describes them, and then begs his auditors to "come to God." It is then, when there is a pause waiting for the advent of the "trail hit-

ters," that the evangelist's musical director begins
playing a plaintive, appealing old hymn. Usually
three or four women, sobbing, rise and start
down the aisle. They are "trail hitting," and as
they walk along the voices of the choir rise and
men start down the aisle. To those who sit back,
half fascinated, Mr. Sunday shouts, "Are you
coming? Jesus is here; come to him!" Others
stand and start toward the evangelist, and before
many moments those who are still in their seats
are conspicuous. It is apparent that they are determined to be wicked, come what may, and in
a few moments they—most of them—join the
throng on the trail. That is an appeal to the
emotions of various kinds. First, fear of future
punishment is invoked; then the emotions awakened by plaintive music and a tender hymn; then
comes that mysterious influence of sympathy with
the sobbing women, while the music continues to
influence the heart. Finally there is the appeal
by the contagion of his own earnestness coupled
with the unwillingness of men to have their un-
belief made conspicuously public. They prefer to
mislead him rather than be labeled "hardened
sinners."

Turning now to the counsel of a man long
honored as a "pastor and teacher": * "The spirituality of the Christian religion implies that the
worshipper is brought into communion with God

* Oswald Dykes, "Duties of a Minister," p. 191.

' in spirit and in truth '—not, that is to say, by the aid of sensuous or material symbols . . . but through the word addressed to the reason and the conscience. In harmony with this must the preacher also commend himself by the manifestation of the truth to every man's conscience. In other words it is on the naked force of religious and moral truth that he must rely. Efforts to play upon the passions except through the understanding are unworthy of the Gospel. Even appeals to the imagination through the senses merely are out of keeping with it. For ecstasies and tumultuous conditions of the soul, created by a heated fancy under the excitement of numbers, have merely a momentary effect and do not produce those permanent ethical results at which the Gospel aims . . . the preacher may agitate the soul of the sinner . . . but the means to be employed must always be moral and spiritual truth, not adventitious nor meretricious aid from harrowing pictures of physical torment, the exhibition of a crucifix to the eye, even sensuous details of the Passion, or the mere influence of the falsetto voice."

With two so diverse ideas from two so prominent preachers it will not be unimportant to give some careful thought to the general subject of *motives*. It may be better at the outset for me to say that in my own judgment neither of these views has the whole truth nor is destitute of truth.

There is truth in both—and error in both—
whether I justify my view you must judge after
you have learned my reasons.

What is a motive? All action is directly produced in response to the command of the soul.
What we call the " will to do " originates in the
soul's " feeling." Some emotional awakening goes
before the doing or saying. Some kind of feeling, in some degree, is back of every conscious
movement of the body, or every word thought-
fully spoken, or every determination to do. This
feeling is always the soul seeking its own comple-
tion or defending its own possessions. If, therefore, one man would cause another to act he must
by some agency awaken an interest—stir the feel-
ing-life by some appeal to the self-interest.

When there is presented to the soul any object
that, if it were possessed, would add to comfort
or self-completion, there arises at once a desire to
get it. That desire is the " moving force " which
lies back of all action—that is the *" motive."*
Note that " motive " does not mean the thing desired, but the awakened desire. Thus money is
not a " motive." In some men it awakens " motive," in others it does not. Reputation is not a
" motive," but in some men reputation awakens a
" motive." If a man seriously desires money,
then showing him a way to get money will stir
all his activities. If he hungers for reputation,
show him how to become famous and he will do

almost anything to get his name in the papers. Thus we see that only those objects that are congruous with a man's nature or character awaken any "motive."

Application of this definition. If you can present any object or any truth, or show any path of life that will add to what one likes and desires, a motive will at once arise. E.g., if a man feels himself a great sinner and is troubled about it, and you present to his mind a gospel that will promise him forgiveness and victory, he will seek to get it. But if he has no sense of sin he will say, as a young man once said to me when I approached him about the Christian faith, "I appreciate your interest in me but really I have no need of it." The Savior said, "They that are well have no need of a physician." His preaching about salvation found no response in the self-righteous Pharisee. But the common people, conscious of their need, heard him gladly. So in trying to persuade men to accept the Christian way of action, thought and hope, the minister must be a student of their desires. Some common meeting ground where to the hungerings of their souls can be offered the *"bread of life."*

Good and bad motives. It is very generally agreed that there are both good and bad motives. But it is not so generally agreed what ones are good and what ones are bad. Some are satisfied

to say that any motive that sets men in motion
to do some good thing is a good motive. " The
end," they say, " justifies the means." " If you
want to get men to ' strike the trail,' whatever
gets them to thus commit themselves to the
Christian life and join the procession of Christians is a legitimate motive." Carried to the extreme this leads to the Jesuit doctrine that even
a lie in a good cause loses its taint of sin if it aims
at a good result. Paul expressed his view on this
when he said of such teachers, " *Their damnation
is just.*" This " Gospel of Expediency " has a
very wide following. I am concerned just now
only with it as it comes into view in preaching. Can we say with wisdom that any appeal to
any motive is good if its aim is to lead men to
do good? Is it best to do as Mr. Sunday is said
above to do, provided it gets men to " strike the
trail"? Does the minister need fumigating for
wickedness after he has made an appeal to a low
motive if his appeal secured a large missionary
collection? Are members of churches unworthy
if they are induced to " come in " by personal affection for the minister? It is evident from what
has been quoted above that on this there is great
divergence of view. The Jansenists * followed the
principle that in teaching no appeal could legiti-
mately be made to any motive except that which

* The managers of a school about 1650 at Port Royal, a
village about eighteen miles from Paris.

arises from the desire to conform to a holy standard of right—to do right just because it is right. No good result would, in their judgment, modify or hide a bad quality in a motive, but on the contrary a result otherwise good is tainted, if not utterly condemned, if it was secured by appeals to a motive other than a sense of duty. Under this idea no appeal can be made except to men's sense of duty to God. " You ought to be a Christian because God wants you to be one." " You ought to do this or that because it is right for you to do so." All other motives are to greater or less degree improper and, in some sense, bad motives. The " naked truth" as quoted above must be the persuading thing. The " sword of the spirit which is the word of God " must be the only weapon. This question is well worthy great consideration. As I have said my own view lies between these—and drawing from each important principles.

The fundamental principle. I should assume that my work as a minister is in the last analysis to build up in men Christian character, and in society the natural application of Christian character to the community life. The individual is first in importance, as the single dollar is the basis of commercial values. A " fiat " Christian is no better than a " fiat " dollar. If the dollar is depreciated all values shrink. If the Christian man shrinks the Christian community shrinks. It is not so much to get good things done as it is to get the doers to be good.

Let me dwell upon that for a moment. When a young man is learning a trade his instructor has an interest in every piece of work done, but the dominant interest is that the apprentice should learn to do good work. The music teacher is pleased when the pupil sings well, but he is not so much concerned that the music be good as that the pupil become a good singer. The Christian is learning the trade and the minister is a " laborer with God " in teaching him the trade—he wants him to attend church, to give to missions, to be peaceable and honest for the sake of these things, but chiefly he wants him *to know the trade* of being a good Christian and *working at it* cheerfully. The Christian is learning the music of the kingdom, but the great aim of the pastor is not to hear some kingdom tunes but to make him a kingdom singer. This I assume is the dominant purpose of the minister.

The good motive. Every intelligent act leaves a residuum of character in the actor. As leaves, that come and then fall, all leave behind them a contribution to the growth of the tree, making its limbs longer and its trunk larger, so every exercise of the will and every movement of the emotions makes its contribution to the upbuilding of the soul in some direction. If, therefore, lower motives are more often or more thoroughly aroused than the higher ones, the soul becomes more full in that direction. If these appeals for good aims are made to the lower and inferior motives, the residuum is low; the increment to the soul is second-class, and the result on the main purpose of preaching is second-class. In determining, therefore, which motives we may wisely enlist, we see that the decision rests on the basis of its residuum of character. Those being the good motives that leave the doer of actions a better Christian for having done them; the sayer of good things a better person for having said them; the donor of money a better man for the giving; and a bad motive being one that while it may secure a desirable result leaves the doer with a greater balance of low elements in his character.

The resultant judgment. You will see here that while one set of men value the objective results of actions and care little for the means by which they are procured and another set value only the motives that prompt to the action, the view that I should take is that both motives and results are valuable and should be considered in determining the course for the minister to follow. Our Creator made us susceptible to these various motives. Each one has its value at times. Life is completest when the whole man is involved. It would be good to secure a large missionary collection by an appeal simply to the sense of obligation to give. But how much better it would be if in getting the collection the donors were led to give from intelligent interest in the world's uplift, and from a feeling of delight in being partners with God and with other men in carrying the gospel to those living in darkness.

Bearing upon this matter it will be of interest to learn the judgment of a leading writer upon ethics. Professor John Dewey, speaking of motives, says: " The first quality which is the object of judgment primarily resides in intention; in the consequences which are foreseen and desired. Ultimately it resides in the disposition or characteristics of a person which are responsible for his foreseeing and desiring just such consequences rather than others." This being true, the minister's task is to reach the disposition and characteristics that determine the act, and so shape them that the results will be worthy of approval.

XII.

I beseech you by the mercies of God.—ROM. 12:1.

MOTIVES (*Continued*)

SINCE we have seen that motives of various kinds are legitimate if along with good results the net residuum of good in the character is conserved, we are to consider some of the available motives to which we may appeal.

These motives with all their varied possibilities of power lie asleep until some bugle call awakens them to action. It is our task to awaken and use them. A studious examination of ourselves shows that truth in some way presented to the mind is the bugle call to which they each respond with alacrity.

Fear. Perhaps, owing to the history of preaching, the first one that comes into mind is fear of various sorts. There are three kinds of fear that have a close relation to religious life. The fear of future punishment is one. In the past that has been the most prominent. Very early the church developed that to the utmost. The paintings of "great masters" presented physical torments with such a seeming relish that it suggests they were fit candidates for it themselves. Mr.

Beecher once said, "*Any one who is willing to be damned for Adam's sin ought to be.*" And those who can revel in the imaginations of such things as figure in early church paintings and are threatened in "orthodox" teachings of past centuries are either devilish in their dispositions or hypocritical in their statements. But at the same time, both the apostles and their great teacher appealed to the fear of some future punishment. Paul wrote that, "Every one must give account of himself to God"; and that, "God will render to every man according to his works . . . tribulation and anguish upon every soul of man that worketh evil." (Rom. 2:9.) Peter wrote, "If God spared not the angels . . . he knows how to keep the unrighteous under punishment." (II Peter 2:2, 9.) And Jesus said that the Judge will say, "Depart ye cursed into the eternal fire which is prepared for the devil and his angels." (Matt. 25:41.) No Bible-believing man can read these things and deny the inevitable sorrow in the future for some of mankind. And if a minister feels this danger threatens any of his congregation he is justified in using this appeal in the earnest and tender spirit that it must beget in a Christ-like man. Godly fear can be aroused only by such a presentation of the danger that lies in the path of wrongdoing as will convince men of its reality. Dogmatic statements about it have little weight. If one can somehow get a foothold in men's own experience from which, to show the present results of wrong, he may find it possible to lead the mind on toward the conviction that its penalties are not exhausted here.

But it is a difficult task. The greater part of our work in this direction lies in keeping the positive teaching of Jesus on the subject always in mind. Mr. Beecher used to say that he always preached with a background of judgment. We must faithfully present the "whole counsel of God," and trust that the Spirit will use it to convince men of their needs.

But to pour forth, as some do, condemnations to "hell" with an unction that seems to indicate that they enjoy doing so not only does no good to others but is a sure sign that such speakers are in great danger of it themselves. No good man can joke about it nor revel in it.

Another kind of fear is that which comes from the idea that "judgments" come upon men here when they do wrong. It is true that if Jesus has undertaken to "present his people without spot or wrinkle" he will do so. If it takes sorrows and disappointments to attain the result they will be sent. But the minister is not wise enough to discriminate between "judgments" and "chastening." His appeals must be general.

Another fear is that which arises from the dread of self-condemnation. To stand before the glass and look ourselves in the eye and know that we are following lower ideals than we might is, to most of us, a great fear. For myself, I did not have any fear of "hell" or of temporal "judgments" when I committed myself to the Christian life. But I did awake to the fact that with the best of Christian influences around me from my youth, and the full blaze of knowledge shining upon me from the Bible and the pulpit and the Christian people, I was following too low ideals—and that moved me. I think that motive is more worthy than the fears of which I have spoken above.

Gratitude. Gratitude is a sense of obligation to make return for blessings. It awakens when the mercies of God have been shown or called to remembrance. Thus Paul wrote, after having shown by careful argument the gracious plan of salvation, "I beseech you, therefore, by the mercies of God (which I have just shown you), present your bodies living sacrifices, holy, acceptable to God, which is your reasonable service." (Rom. 12:1.) The Psalmist understood this when he wrote, "Bless the Lord, O my soul, and all that is within me bless his holy name; bless the Lord, O my soul, and forget not all his benefits; who forgiveth all thine iniquities; who healeth all thy diseases; who crowneth thee with lovingkindness and tender mercies." The Psalmist said, "What shall I render unto the Lord for all his benefits toward me? I will take the cup of

salvation and call upon the name of the Lord."
(Ps. 116: 13.) It awakens this motive to relate
and exalt the " benefits toward us." To do that
is a most worthy appeal. A college mate of mine
was the son of a most worthy woman, who became
a widow when my friend was a small boy. He
was brought up wisely by his mother. He was
industrious, clean, kind, honest, capable. The
neighbors said, " Why, he is as good as any
church member. Why should he be a Christian?" and what was quite different, he thought
so himself. But in the good pleasure of him who
sent his spirit to show us truth this young man
who thought so highly of himself came one day
to see himself in a different light. He said to
me, " I saw that all my excellence of reputation
was due to Christ whose word I had been taught,
whose people had surrounded me with holy influences; whose saint, my mother, had taught me by
precept and example; and I had done nothing but
receive all this with not a thrill of gratitude to
him; and I seemed to myself to be the most
unworthy of all the young men in Lowell, Mass."
Gratitude arose in him and moved him to a very
consecrated Christian life. This motive is one
that exalts a man. To give money or time or
effort to any good cause from that motive leaves
a residuum in the character of rare value.

Self-respect. Whatever others may think of us
we must think well of ourselves. Every man has

that in him, and to show him that any actions will
give him just ground to respect himself is a great
and worthy appeal. To tell men in a dictatorial
way that they are only " unworthy worms of the
dirt "; that they are " born in sin and conceived in
iniquity," and that only the great mercy of God
can afford them any ground of hope,—while they
may themselves often feel that to be their case, it
is never good nor wise for others in an appeal for
a better life to tell them so. It is the business of
the Spirit of God to convict of sin. He will
wound. We must bind up. He may plough the
heart; we must sow the seed and cultivate it.
Most men know their sins. Many do not know the
remedy. John wrote, " Beloved now are we the
Sons of God and it is not yet made manifest what
we shall be. We know that if he shall be mani-
fested we shall be like him; for we shall see him
even as he is." And Paul said, " Walk worthy of
your calling." In school no good teacher allows
a pupil to think he is belittled by his teacher.
Many pupils who are oppressed at home by pov-
erty, or unwise parents, have been quickened into
studious scholars by teachers who had the wisdom
to appeal to the self-respect. This appeal is almost
wholly lacking in some of our pulpits. It is fault-
finding most of the time. One hears scolding and
pessimism. The minister means well but he lacks
the pedagogical tact to make his appeal to the
motive of self-respect. Jesus taught, not that we

are the offscouring of the world, but the "*light of the world,*" set up on a candlestick to give light unto all that are in the house. Therefore, do not let your light be of the wrong sort, but of the sort that leads men to glorify God.

The Psalmist said, " When I behold the heavens, the work of thy hands, what a wondrous being is man that thou art mindful of him." *

Shame to fail in duty. President Wilson gives us an illustration of this in his communication of July 12, 1917. Seeking to check speculation in food, and getting rich out of the war while men were giving their lives to help Europe, he did not scourge the public as though he dealt with slaves. He did not, Kaiser fashion, assume that he and God jointly owned them. He did not call them " my people " nor Satan's people; but addressed them, " My fellow countrymen. . . . " In these days when we are sending hundreds of thousands of our young men across the seas to serve a great cause, no true man who stays behind to work for them and sustain them by his labor will ask himself what he is going to make out of that labor. . . . He will give as freely and with as unstinted sacrifice as they. . . . I take it for granted that those who argue otherwise do not stop to think what that means. Do they mean that you must be paid, must be bribed to make

* Read in line with this the book, " The Passing of the Third Floor Back " (J. K. Jerome), and " The Gospel of Good Will " (Pres. W. D. Hyde).

your contribution—that costs you neither a drop of blood nor a tear when the whole world is in travail? . . . Do you mean that you will exact a price and drive a bargain with the men who are enduring the agony of this war on the battle-field . . . before you will come forward and do your duty and give some part of your life . . . for the things we are fighting for? . . . You know, and I know what response you will make . . . not that I have any fear as to the result."

Material advantage. It is not wrong to teach men the importance of prosperity in business—but to promise money profit for the exercise of Christian charity is to belie the cause. Jacob sought to dicker with God. He said, "If you will prosper me I will give you a tithe." That is, "If you give me a dollar's worth of prosperity I will give you ten per cent." To make a plea now for gifts to Christian work on the promise that you will be prospered in business is to Jacobize men—from which good Lord deliver us all. The cause of missions and of religion is worthy a better plea. Response to such would only leave a residuum of covetousness.

But I need not continue. It would prolong the discussion to mention love of country, love of the church, love of the brethren, desire for heaven, love of Christ. The great principle of control is, Motives that secure desirable results and leave a residuum of good in the character

are always worthy, all others are not. It is true
that the prophet Malachi wrote, "Bring ye all
the tithes into the storehouse, that there may be
meat in my house, and prove me, saith the Lord
of hosts, if I will not open the windows of heaven
and pour you out a blessing, that there is not
room enough to receive it." (Mal. 3:10.) But
that was rather as a test of their faithfulness than
an appeal to their greed. And even that is not
without the inquiry whether the tithing system
did not lie at the root of the selfish covetousness
that has marked and damaged the Jewish race ever
since. A rich man once told me that tithing made
him stingy. He was always figuring how much he
could give and not trench on his own nine-tenths.

Usefulness. This appeals to those who have
already some culture in the Christian life. Moses
asked his father-in-law to join the Israelites. He
said, "Come with us and we will do you good."
But Hobab replied, "O I am very contented
where I am." Then Moses said, "We need you
for our guide in the wilderness." "Well, then,
I will go." It would be unwise to say to men
that the cause of Christ "needs" them, but it
touches some of the best springs of action to
show people how they can be useful. To say to
a young man, "You have the gift of leadership
and can bring others with you"; or to a woman,
"If you will do so and so it will carry this movement to success"; or this man of means, "If you

will lead off this debt can be paid; or this new activity of the church can be launched." These and many similar appeals are not only legitimate but very effective with the better sort of people.

Authority. Some teachers insist that an appeal to authority is not a worthy one. It is said that the integrity of our own personality is endangered when we say to men, "You are under obligation to do this because God says you are to do it. It is not for you to ask why, but to obey, and the scripture is quoted: "To obey is better than sacrifice and to hearken than the fat of rams." These say: "That only is truly ethical which a man does because his own mind and heart so approve it that he acts from his own center. His will coalesces with the divine will as two drops of water melt into one. There is no doubt that such harmony of will existed between Jesus and his Father. But as a matter of fact it does not so exist between us and the Father.

To me the appeal to authority of God as a reason why we should do any act is the first and natural appeal to make to those who are immature in knowledge and experience. I think that to obey God just because he is God is to learn the excellencies of his ways and ultimately come to do his will from spontaneous desire. Ruskin somewhere said that we learn to love the right by doing it, and until we do love it we are not in a mature ethical state.

XIII.

EXPOSITION

THE Bible is the great source of knowledge and instruction in the Christian religion. We do not by any means say the *only* source. Nor is it the most reliable source in *all* religious matters. Nature and history are sources that antedate and outrank the Bible in fundamental things. There was longing for God before there were any altars or temples.

"The groves were God's first temples." There was revelation, and faith in it, long before any book of our Bible was written. Abraham came out from Ur guided, we do not know how. Human hearts now have their longings and their faith where there is no Bible. But nevertheless the Christian faith and the Christian hope grow in the soil of Bible knowledge. The foundations precede them, but the building is from teaching found only in the New Testament. There is "religion" in abundance where there is no "gospel," but the hearts of men are not *satisfied* until the gospel message reaches them.

144

"Exposition" is bringing to men's view what is inside of that book. Since the Bible is the standard by which our teaching is measured, and the real source of our knowledge of the distinctively Christian truth, it is of first importance that the contents of that book be made known to the people. The pastor's privilege and duty is to search for its doctrine and its promises and its ideals; and, having found them, to bring them to the people. The spies were sent up to examine the land of Canaan, and report back to Moses and Israel their discoveries, so that the people might be encouraged to face the journey to that promised and longed-for land. They brought back specimens of the fruit. They said, "It is a goodly land: it has many and strong inhabitants but we shall be able to overcome them."

So the pastor is to explore the chapters of biblical history and survey the blessings promised to the faithful; he is to study the routes of life along which the good have travelled, and bring to his people not only the story of the country but some of its fruits. To do that is what is meant by "exposition."

The scripture thus opened is the great source of many things. Paul said, "It is profitable for teaching, for reproof, for correction, for instruction which is in righteousness; that the man of God may be complete, furnished completely unto every good work." (II Tim. 3:16.)

In educating a community no single agency is equal in value to a sympathetic, intelligent unfolding of the scripture.

A great danger. I have said in another place that the allegorical interpretation has more to be said for it and more against it than can well be enumerated. In exposition this method finds its field. The idea of that method is that the words, the events, the persons of the Old Testament, and to a large extent the same in the New Testament, carry a double sense. They are "earthly stories with heavenly meanings." People with active imaginations see almost anything in the scripture when they skillfully use that sort of a glass to look through. And like a kaleidoscope the meaning changes every time the glass passes to a new beholder.

As one has said, "The Bible has been treated as a magazine of curious and mystical analogies; as a work on geology, anticipating the labors of Hitchcock and Dana and Agassiz; as a dictionary of moral precepts, all of which were of equal and uniform validity; as a sort of a divine puzzle, whose parts could be put together to spell out some theurgic symbol of salvation. Lyric metaphors have been made over into studies in science. Inspiring poems have been treated as prosaic biographies. Parables and visions have been boiled down into accounts of historical occurrences. Figures and allusions to seven horns and seven eyes have been made to refer to events like an eclipse of the sun in Germany, or the election of a President in the United States. The fusion of two metals in the temple has taught the humanity and divinity of Christ. The five stones in David's sling have been made to spell J-E S-U-S. A scarlet cloth on the walls of Jericho has been a prophecy of the blood of the New Covenant. Coverings of the tabernacle have taught the doctrine of imputed righteousness. Riddles, conundrums, recondite and strained interpretations have been found on all its pages. Like a child's box of letters, it has furnished amusement to renowned scholars who have tried to see how much they could " spell out " by means of its verses." *

On the other hand, what a wonderful adaptation the book has for such uses. The New Testament itself has some passages that suggest the allegorical character of parts of the Old Testament, so that in spite of the fanciful things said by some to be taught by it, we cannot say it is all fancy.

Whatever the preacher may do with texts, the *teacher,* the true pastor, will want to avoid fancies, but he will also want to utilize the book. There are several principles to guide us. First, the *purpose of the writer or speaker of any passage must be found.* For example, when the Psalmist wrote his hymn—say the 105th Psalm—was he teaching the details of history? Certainly not.

* Rev. George H. Ferris, Philadelphia.

He was showing the guidance that God had given to Israel. He was concerned with making Israel know that God was their God, and that he wanted them to "keep his laws." He wrote not to preserve history but to promote holiness.

The author of the "Gospel of Matthew" was not writing a life of Christ, nor the writer of Acts a life of Peter or of Paul. The first was giving a summary of Jesus' teaching and the saving deeds of his life. The other was showing how the gospel spread over the world, and how its simple message to some Jewish peasants was expanded to take in the philosophers of Athens, and the politicians of Rome, and the rest of the world. Paul's letters were not written primarily for the instruction of Americans but for the comfort and help of his own generation.

If you are to teach thoughtful people you must have that conception underneath all your exposition. Other folks have found that out, and you must accept that point of view.

The second principle is: *Seek the purpose of those who put these particular books of the Bible into the collection of sacred books.*

Why, for example, are Paul's letters written to some one else put in here? Why, out of all the things that Jesus did, were these preserved? In answer to these questions we may say that the dominating purpose was to show us the path of life and help us walk in it, by showing us the

inner life of those who did walk in it and of those
who did not walk in it. It was not to make us
know the facts of David's life that his story was
told so much as to show us the spirit he had. It
was not to tell us how bad a woman Jezebel was—
we have bad women now—but to show us how
God defeated her. The story of Israel's journey
through the wilderness has no value in its details—no one goes over that route now—but it
shows how God guides us through a longer wilderness to a better Canaan. Therefore, in teaching truth from this book, we are to look for the
moral situation back of the events and set that
forth. The Twenty-third Psalm shows how a
godly man feels toward his God. The story of
Peter's denial shows how a sensitive spirit may
flinch at the reproach of men, and yet under the
love of Christ may recover great courage. The
story of Lazarus is not important in its details.
Whether he died again or what he said about his
four days in the grave has no spiritual value, but
it shows how Jesus can call back our "buried
selves." How

> "Down in the human heart,
>   Crushed by the tempter,
> Feelings lie buried
>   That grace can restore."

The story of Paul's conversion is not important
except that it gives us the key to all Christian

life. Paul said, " I was not disobedient to the
heavenly vision." All the rest followed naturally.
It does not matter whether the Prodigal Son went
to Egypt or Rome in his wanderings; but it is
of great value to know that his father loved him
and forgave him; and that Jesus made that father
the miniature of Our Father in Heaven. The
mysterious figures that act in the drama of The
Revelation are forever useless to us, but the story
of battle between Christ's kingdom and its ene-
mies, followed by victory and peace—not " peace
without victory "—is a great comfort to us all.
So through all the book the faith, the courage, the
patience of men are the elements of value for the
teaching of which the books have been exalted
and preserved.

The third principle is : *We must interpret by the
same rules as any other writing dealing with the
same subjects*. There is no " sacred rhetoric "
any more than there is sacred arithmetic. The
rules of rhetoric are the same whether we read a
poem by Milton or David. The rules of logic are
the same whether we follow Paul in Romans or
Socrates. This is too often ignored or forgotten.
Some of the Bible is poetry and must be read as
such, some of it is commandment and must be
obeyed as such.

To teach as the language of prophecy what was
only the language of desire or faith is to mis-
interpret the word. Foresight is very different

from faith. When Isaiah wrote Chapter 2: 3-4, he was not *seeing* the future; he was describing the sure result that would follow when men should go up to the house of the Lord to learn his ways and be willing to walk in his paths. They have not all done this yet; otherwise we should not have the war which grieves the heart of all but the German " war lords " who make a living by it. All this requires familiarity with the historical situation and with the religious needs of that time. It will be no small part of preparation for exposition to be able to sketch the situation morally and historically in swift clear way, so that you may introduce the audience to the circumstances that give character to the passage. There are some passages that are like diamonds, beautiful in themselves. But many more that depend upon their setting.

You can teach and educate a people in more ways and on more subjects and with greater profit to all by expositions of Bible passages than by any other method. It will require study but it will pay for the study. There are occasions when you will need to discuss themes that belong to the civil conditions of your people; but this book contains even for such themes the richest mines of the truth needed for such occasions.

The story of Boaz and his laborers has its lesson for the employer.

The story of Nebuchadnezzar tells rulers not to

be lifted up in their successes. The story in II Kings 12: 4-12 tells us the unwisdom of committing great works to officials without oversight and reports of their stewardship. The rebellion against Solomon because of his severity and extravagancies recalls the saying of Mr. Lincoln, " You cannot fool all the people all the time." Indignation may be dammed up for a time, but it will accumulate to the overthrow of the wicked. We are seeing now how at last—at last, after generations of patient delay—the rum-seller class is to be overthrown as thoroughly as it has been for a long time despised.

A broad study of the sociology of the biblical history gives us a view of underlying principles that must come sooner or later into control of our community life. These principles had only fitful expression in that old-time history, but they are there. The prophecies of Amos and Isaiah and Malachi are rich in warnings against the evils of trusts that are selfish, and of ecclesiastical dominance and religious indifference. One cannot read those prophecies without being impressed with the vital relation between ethical conduct in social affairs and religious healthfulness. Ceremonialism has no honor before the denunciations of those men of God.

XIV.

Exhort with all longsuffering and doctrine.
II Tim. 4:2.
*I cease not to pray that ye may know what is
the hope of his calling; what the riches of the
glory of his inheritance in the Saints, and
what the exceeding greatness of his power
toward us.*—Eph. 1:18, 19.

DOCTRINAL TEACHING

NO full-orbed education can be secured without doctrinal knowledge. Paul in his
prayers for the Ephesians asked that they might
come to *know* the "hope of their calling," the
"glory of their inheritance," and the "power of
God toward them." Those were the great doctrines or teachings. Doctrines are not speculations of the philosophic minds, nor the fancies of
the imaginative, nor the discussions of petty denominational matters. Doctrines are the orderly
statement of facts. They are lists of what God
has done, is doing, and proposes to do for those
who commit themselves to his care and guidance.
Doctrines describe the glorious privileges and possibilities that lie before the Christian as a country
to be possessed—a fair Canaan "where their possessions lie." Doctrine teaches what resources
of divine help we have in our journey to those

possessions. The prayer of Paul was comprehensive and orderly. When he asked that the Ephesians might know the hope, the glory, and the power, he covered all the doctrinal field.

All men have "doctrine" of some sort. If you ask any thoughtful Christian why he faces the world so bravely and meets trouble so triumphantly, he will tell you it is because of the anticipation of "things to come." He is "saved by hope" and "hope that is seen is not hope. But if we hope for that which is not seen, then do we with patience wait for it."

If you ask him why he loves the company of the Christian people more than others, and why he is willing, if need be, to "suffer affliction with the people of God," he replies that the glory of the church, which is the Lord's "inheritance," is greater to him than "all the treasures of Egypt." And if you tell him he will not be able to maintain himself in the Christian life, but that his own moral weakness will prevent his final victory, he will tell you that the power of God is his re-enforcement, and "he who has begun a good work in him will carry it on until the day of Jesus Christ."

All these confidences which give him strength and gladness are the results of his doctrine of Christ. That is, knowing the facts about God's interest in him and readiness to help him, he is buoyed up by these great truths, taught in the

Bible progressively from the simple faith of Abel and Abraham on to the maturer knowledge given us in the New Testament.

This fact if well considered will help you to get past the stumbling blocks that acrimonious discussions of mysterious or unimportant things have put in the path. It will strip doctrinal preaching of the disfiguring and sometimes poisonous vines that have overrun it, and reveal to you the unsuspected beauty of the architecture. Doctrine will be to your people like the rains of summer which, in cold climates, soak into the deep ground and supply the springs in winter when rains do not come. These doctrinal instructions must be fundamental. Paul's prayer well indicates the general divisions; namely, what things has the Christian a right to hope for? What are the glories that belong to the church? What help is available in the conflict with sin and death? You will find your own spirit will be refreshed by the search for the reply to these questions, and as you tell to others what you have found you will be entrenching them in their faith.

How shall we proceed? If you can make or buy a true doctrinal catechism for your families and Sunday School teachers to use do so. It will lay the " bottom courses " of their future faith deep and solid.

Do not get one that deals with the " secret

decrees" of God. If they are "secret" it is
ill-mannered as well as useless to pry into
them.

Do not get one that attempts to explain all the
ways of God. For Jesus said some of the great
things are like the wind that bloweth. We cannot tell whence they come, nor whither they go.
We know them by their results.

Get one that classifies the teachings of the
book in orderly fashion and confines itself to
what is capable of being wrought into our daily
life, such as will promote "love, joy, peace, longsuffering, gentleness, goodness, meekness, tem-
perance, faith."

Have a system in your work. The "Christian
year" gives a good framework. This covers the
ground of Jesus' life, work, and teachings. I
have followed that some years without any an-
nouncements to the congregation. This guards
against keeping in a doctrinal rut.

A friend of mine tells me he has been following for several months the theme, "What Christ
is to the world." He has had sermons on Christ's
value to the sinful, and to the struggling, and to
governments, and to literature, and to ethical culture, and to parents, and to the dying. In this
way his congregation must have unconsciously
been enriched by large veins of Christ, and that
is always the fertilization of the soil in which the
fruits of the Spirit grow.

Once in my early ministry, while I was studying theology for myself apart from the seminary training, I followed the line followed in the book I was trying to master. I have reason to think that those sermons given forty years ago are bearing fruit in that community now. A great doctrinal truth once implanted never exhausts its influence on the life.

But especially fill yourself with contemplation of large themes. To become a mere picker-out of details is not inspiring. You will have some folk that will want you to give them codes to live by instead of principles. They will want *you* to tell them how to regulate their family matters and their family devotions instead of seeking Christ's idea. They do not want to think, or perhaps they do not know how to do so. At any rate they want you to think for them. Sometimes you will need to do so but as far as possible keep to large themes. My college president used to say to us, " Do not have a small study, it will cramp your thought." We have all had the experience of being cramped in thought, perplexed about some question of duty, and then we took up a book of large things, like Paul's letter to the Ephesians, and it took us up into the mountains from which we could get our bearings and untangle our minds from the devious ways through the lowlands of our thinking.

Paul, before he ventured to mention details

of duty, took his readers up into the mountains. For example, in Ephesians he has given us the inventory of the Christian's wealth in chapter 1:1-14. Then he has told them of the "exceeding greatness of his power toward us," in that he raised Christ from the dead (1:19). Then he reminded them how when they were "dead" Christ had "quickened them" (2:5), and that now they were all "builded together for an habitation of God" (2:22). Then, and not until then, he turns to details, "Therefore, I beseech you to walk worthy of the vocation wherewith ye are called" (4:1).

In Galatians he tells them how he who had all there is in family birth and in ceremonial excellence was blind to the glory of Jesus (1:13). But God revealed his son in him (1:16) and taught him that the way of life is never closed to people of faith, but that like Abraham we "all are children of God by faith in Christ Jesus" (3:26) and are redeemed from the bondage of ceremony. *Then,* and not until then, he says, "*Therefore* stand fast in the liberty wherewith Christ has set us free" (5:1). Thus he goes on to tell us about the "fruit of the spirit" (5:22).

So the great preachers whose work has shaped the current of thought and life in great communities have been those whose doctrinal teaching has been large and high and commanding.

" Go thou and do likewise."

This at once raises the questions, *What doctrines shall we teach?* It is not my purpose here to discuss disputed subjects. Nor to prescribe a set of doctrines for any one. What I want to impress on every one is that he have some well-digested system of doctrines which he has verified, to some extent at least, in his own experience, or that are verifiable in experience; doctrines that have a real worth in making men better men; and that he teach these with great care and ardor. Personally—and I may not be wise in this—there is no value in discussing the time when Christ is to return or the condition of the world when he comes. Either view can be made to appear correct by manipulation of the scripture. The earliest Christians were not only ignorant about it but some of them were in error. Paul himself did not make it so evident that good men can agree concerning his view. What we are sure of is that we are to teach men everywhere to commit themselves to Christ, to do his will, to love their fellow men, and God supremely. Of these there is no question. I should leave the other themes out of the doctrinal scheme for general instruction. Even what are called denominational discussions profit but little and convert few. There are times when such should be taught to the people but never controversially. But as I have said this may be due only to my personal lack of interest in such semi-speculative matters.

When men asked Jesus whether few are to be saved he replied, Strive to enter the narrow gate. When people were disturbed about the time of Jesus' return, Paul said, Be not disturbed about it for it will come without warning. And Jesus himself said he did not know; but that only his Father knows. Just how the death of Jesus affected things at the upper end of God's ladder of salvation no one knows. We only know that, as Jacob knew the ladder he saw had God at the upper end, so the work of Jesus met all the requirement, and now the way is open for help and salvation to every one that will believe on him.

The atonement is now and always has been a mysterious fact. The substitutionary view was preached for centuries with great results for good. The moral influence view has been accepted by thousands of sincere and self-sacrificing men. Some of the best culture of the age has been influenced by such teachers. It would be a grievous error to deny to either set of teachers their place in the Christian fold or the Christian ministry. But one must have his own conviction and must preach, then, with positiveness. It is not necessary that he be uncharitable or controversial in his presentation. Every one must give account of himself, and that account not to men but to God.

XV

CREEDS AND LITURGIES

IN former chapters we have noticed how the great agency for moving the will of men is a knowledge of the truth. The didatic sermon, however, does not go directly to the audience chamber of the soul but must go around by way of the emotional entrance. But when Truth is clearly seen it moves the deepest emotions, and holds its influence longer than any other agency. Once convince a man of a great truth that affects his life for the better and you have "stirred a fountain whose waters never more will rest." For such a man the helm is lashed so that no storms can wrench it from its place. The course is set not by the compass of immediate desire, that may be deflected by passing temptations, but by the stars of heaven. In this chapter I wish to speak of Creeds and Liturgies in their relation to teaching of the truth. At the outset we must clear up the definition of these words "creed" and "liturgy."

By "creed" we mean the formal statement of fundamental religious truth. We do not mean something that by believing it or assenting to it, a man becomes a member of the kingdom of heaven, a sort of password that admits him without further inquiry to the company of the " elect." It is only a statement of what we think is the truth. An opening up to the public of our inner convictions, both for their good and for the continual correction of our own faith. In the early centuries—between the third and the sixteenth—the dominant church taught, and probably most people believed, that there was a mystical power in the sacraments by which those who received them became children of God and thus of the kingdom of heaven. But that was very deficient both in theory and results. The Reformation, while keeping much of the sacramental idea, gave an important emphasis to the intellectual requirements. The *knowledge* of the truth and acceptance of it was made the more important thing. This placed great value upon the careful statement of the truth. For if a man does really accept any great truth—he is, therefore, compelled by his own thinking processes to accept the necessary inferences from it. For example, if a man is thoroughly convinced that Paul was an inspired, authoritative teacher, he must feel bound by all that Paul taught. If a man really believes that God orders all things from the beginning he cannot, if he would, escape the conclusions that Calvin drew from that great promise. Thus the fundamental statements must be carefully drawn, or erroneous inferences will be made. But it soon became evident that a verbal assent was inadequate. Many who assented to the doctrine of the cross in the creed were strangers to the cross in their lives. Men who swore to the creed would swear at everything else. Like those Jews to whom Paul wrote, "The very name of Christ was blasphemed among the Gentiles because of them." They said the "*Credo*" and lived the "*diabolo*." But by "creed" we mean the statements, for pedagogical reasons and uses only, of what we think are fundamental and commonly accepted truths.

Liturgy. Many people who have not given the matter much thought and have not been used to its practical meaning confound "liturgy" with "rite" or "canon." This confounds the subject. *By "liturgy" we mean an established order of services in public worship,* including prayers, hymns, scripture readings. Among the non-liturgical people they are rather loosely called, "order of services" or "preliminaries." For us—as I write to the non-liturgical pastors chiefly—liturgical services are rather underestimated. We have them. They are very solidly established—not by ecclesiastical authority, but by custom of long standing, widely followed.

We have an "Order of Service" chiefly because congregations do not like surprises. They dislike to sing where they are expecting to listen. But the pedagogical value is too important to be thus underestimated. *Liturgies for educational purposes are no modern invention.* The great purpose of the Jewish tabernacle was to teach. It stood in the center of the camp, to show that Jehovah was among them, and they were to guard his shrine. Chosen representatives of the people could approach Jehovah in worship; but the washings and the white garments and the incense all told the simplest mind that those who came to God must have clean hands and pure hearts. Thus the fundamental facts were daily taught through the senses of sight and sound. Later the temple magnified this feature. So that when the queen of Sheba came to visit King Solomon and saw the liturgy she said, " Blessed are thou, and blessed be thy God." The Psalms were used as a part of the liturgy. They were sung by the congregation and by choirs. They praised and prayed; they confessed and they consecrated in these psalms. One who is familiar with them now can find most apt expression for nearly all religious exercises and hopes, except those immediately dependent upon the resurrection of Jesus. The churches' history was drilled into all the nation by the historical psalms like the 104-5-6. They all knew it as Boston knows about Bunker Hill or Philadelphia about the Declaration of Independence. I can but think that we of the more congregational habit might gain in educational power if we would get together and draw upon the combined wisdom of our laymen and ministers to provide a liturgy—not to be imposed upon any church but to be available *voluntarily* for all. I believe it would so commend itself to the good sense and the heart needs that it would soon become quite general. It would represent thus the need of all, rather than the notions of one, and would help toward the ultimate union of Christians. But whether this be done or not, the "order of services" surrenders its chief value if it is not made to teach with elegant repetition the great facts on which our common faith rests, and to furnish suitable forms of expression for our common approaches to God.

The value of common elements in the prayer and praise is seen not only in the use of hymns for the congregation but in the "responsive readings," and in the united utterance of the "Lord's Prayer." I can but think the desire for these is very poorly met in all churches today. The Episcopal service was made in the seventeenth century. Some of its prayers are not in harmony with our thoughts nor suitable to our needs. There is an element of cringing fear of God in parts of it, and a very great lack of interest in specific missionary objects in others. We of this day give the cause of missions and education and Sunday Schools and Evangelism and social service such large place in our prayers that the Prayer

Book is very inadequate indeed. The new Presbyterian liturgy has prayers much more up-to-date. But one feels that while in substance they are adequate they are rather more rhetorical than the " common prayer " should be.

Probably one difficulty in securing any new liturgy grows out of the notion that the " inspired scriptures " are the only safe source of phrases in which to approach our Father in heaven. Without wishing to impeach in the least the " reputation " of the Bible, I think there is no reason to suppose that it was intended for our use in public worship. Men of today are as well able to express their own prayers or praises as they are to select phrases from the Bible and make them into a sort of mosaic that has for its recommendation the fact that its material is all taken from the verses of ancient writings as the huts of natives are built from the stones of ancient Rome. There is, so far as I know, no evidence that Jehovah or Jesus is particular to be addressed in the English language of 1611. And certainly David was not writing his psalms with the idea that they would fit our need. If it were not done with perfectly serious and reverent intent it would seem to be a most foolish exercise to read a psalm that has no connection with our needs; and then make it doubly empty by reading it responsively. There can be no educational value in such reading and certainly there is no worship in it.

The value of a creed in the liturgy. When we seek for some statement that is common to the great majority of the congregation the task is more complex. If we have one it has great value. To repeat it in unison many Sundays in a year fixes it in the minds of the young and refreshens it in the minds of others. It ought in these days to be possible to agree on one. One that has been used with satisfaction is here given:

" We believe in the goodness of God Our Father, maker of heaven and earth, in whose moral image we are made.

" And in Jesus Christ, his only Son, who in our form and nature truly lived and taught among men the things of God; who died for our sins, and was buried; who was raised from the dead by the power of God; who is now exalted as Head over the church, and the One to whom every knee should gladly bow, and whom every tongue should gratefully confess as Lord.

" We believe in the helpful influences of the Holy Spirit.

" We believe in the forgiveness of sin, in the resurrection of the dead, and in the life everlasting.

" We believe in the teachings of the Bible as the safe guide of religious life and the basis of heavenly hopes.

" We believe in the fellowship of Christians in religious work and worship, and in our common duty to preach the gospel to all mankind. And to promote the kingdom of God on earth."

Conclusion of the whole matter. In so complex a matter none of us can be dogmatic; but I am sure that the non-liturgical churches would profit if they would recognize more fully the educational value of liturgy and creed; and set some agency at work to secure, for improving the services in each church, the combined wisdom and skill of all denominations. Meanwhile, the pastor can give consideration to the matter and make the so-called "preliminary services" richer in instruction than they usually are, and more suitable to the aspirations of the church.

Let none of us allow the choir or the fashion of the hour to prevent the fruitful use of the liturgical part of the Sunday worship.

A SUGGESTION FOR AN "ORDER OF SERVICES"

THE PEOPLE'S SERVICE (OR SERVICE OF WORSHIP)

Organ.

Call to worship.	A suitable passage of scripture read by the pastor or leader of the service.
Invocation or The Lord's Prayer.	This should not be a prayer for anything except for God's blessing in the worship of the hour.
A hymn of praise.	All standing.

A **prayer** printed in the hymn book in which **all join.**
The choir.

A confession of faith.	All standing.
A hymn of praise.	" "

The pastoral prayer.

Notices and collection prefaced by suitable words about the
object of it.

THE PASTORAL SERVICE (OR SERVICE OF INSTRUCTION)

Scripture Lesson.
The Sermon.
Prayer and Hymn.
Benediction.

This service, it will be seen, has two parts quite
distinct. The first should be complete in itself.
It should prepare the way but should not antici-
pate the sermon.

The second part should have a central idea in
both scripture and sermon.

XVI.

These things I write unto thee that thou mayest know how thou oughtest to behave thyself in the house of God.—I Tim. 3:15.

PEDAGOGY IN THE MANAGEMENT OF THE CHURCH

I HAVE said that there is an educational element in all the pastoral oversight. Not only is he an educator when he preaches, but in all the general affairs there is an influence that goes out from the way things are organized and directed that shapes the thought of the young and fits them to carry the responsibilities of life in a worthy way.

It is said that the framers of the Bill of Rights in Virginia got their germinal ideas from church government in some New England church. Whether that be true or not, young men learn in the churches where they belong how to live together in the civil relations of life. There is business of a simple sort going on in all churches. Pastors are called, officers elected, delegates chosen, resolutions passed, plans for raising money devised, members received and dismissed, etc., etc. All this implies discussion and votes. It puts upon the church the problem of living together and unifying ideas, submitting to majorities, and keeping the atmosphere of the church sweet and wholesome in it all. Some of the principles that are essential to this are:

The spiritual welfare of the church is of first importance. No special method of work, no personal ambitions, no pet schemes of pastor or of people should outweigh the peaceable, spiritual prosperity of the church. Better be without a new parsonage than have one that costs a split or a seam in the church. Better have the old meeting house and harmony than a fine one with a fuss. It will require the pastor to be himself patient, and ready to heed the counsel of delay rather than hasten his project and divide his flock. If you are the one who is ready to set the example of yielding and putting the peace of the church above your own personal schemes you will not only contribute to the general atmosphere of peace, but it will give you a leverage in your exhortations to others to do the same thing. In this way your younger members will learn the lesson of true community life, the lesson of " give and take," without which people of different tastes cannot live together.

This is especially important because the church is like a city set on a hill. A musical society, a Masonic lodge, a social club, have selected membership and single aims, but a church must take rich and poor, the learned and the unlettered, the old and the young, the male and the female. No such diversity exists in any other organization. But yet it must stand, and it does stand, as the pattern of social management. When you lead your church in such wise and peaceable way, you are not only securing the welfare of the church but you are making a valuable contribution to public education in civil conduct needed for the welfare of our government.

But there are times when one must take a stand against stubborn and narrow-minded men, those who mistake their wish for church welfare and who mistake backbone for conscience and willfulness for wisdom. That will try your mettle. Pray for a loving spirit yourself and remember that you are not the church. Others must share the task and the responsibility of deciding important questions.

Another principle is that the *whole church stand on a common level of membership*. That is, every man and woman of mature age has a right to be heard in all questions of importance, but in the appointed way. There is no aristocracy that may exclude from notice the opinion of humblest man or woman from a fair consideration. To recognize this at all times is a great educating influence in emphasizing the brotherhood of the kingdom.

This does not imply that all are equal in wisdom or efficiency. The old idea is still

the true one—" Thou shalt provide out of all
the people able men, such as fear God, men
of truth, hating covetousness; and place such
over them." (Ex. 18:20.) This was confirmed
in the New Testament times by those who
knew the value of the Old Testament principle.
" Look ye out from among you seven men of
honest report, full of the Holy Spirit and wisdom whom we may appoint over this business."
(Acts 7:3.)

This is the republican form of government. It
puts responsibility upon such as are competent. It
requires them to have the sanction of the church,
and inferentially the hearty support and respect of
the church. No good influence goes out from
" passing honors around." Positions in the
church are not " honors," though they are honor-
able. They are trusts committed, responsibilities
imposed. At the same time it is well to have recur-
ring periods when new men may be asked to take
the work. This gives opportunity to develop new
men and to relieve some of work they have
carried a long time. This is an educative measure
for it not only uses new men but it teaches that
office is not a class distinction. Indeed, the term
" office " is best honored by not using it. Better
say a man is asked to do a certain " work " than
to say he is elected to an " office." An " office "
may become nothing but an " honorary degree "
like D.D. on the pastor; which may signify vari-

ous degrees of honor between a " Dead Dog " and real " Doctor of Divinity."

Another principle is that each member be taught to do his part financially.   Paul wrote, " Let every one of you lay by in store as God has prospered him."   (I Cor. 16.)   " No idlers in the church " is the motto.   Mr. Spurgeon used to say, " All at it, and at it all the time."   It is not left to the pastor to control the financial matters of the church, but he can do his part toward securing a method of support that is both correct in spirit and educational in effect.   The " pew renting " system has one good influence.   It gathers the family in one place and emphasizes the family as a center of religious life.   Any system is deficient that leaves the congregation to scatter promiscuously about the house.   But the fixing of prices on the pews and putting them in public places is bad all the way through.   The evil begins when a stranger enters the vestibule.   He sees there what amounts to a plutocratic chart of the congregation.   Here in those center pews, not too far front, are the " nabobs," up there in the corner are the " bobs " of the church, and over on the sides and rear are the " common folk."

Then the people are tempted to draw the line of wealth, and classify the congregation according to the size of the pew rentals.   That hurts the good nature of the church.

Further than this, the system is seldom successful. It is the most popular failure in the world. It is nearly always supplemented by an appeal in some way to the voluntary contributions of the people, the final resort at the end of the year being to that appeal. As a business affair, if there was no other reason, it should for this be supplanted by the voluntary system.

This latter method should first be constantly attended to by yearly every-member canvass if necessary. Every new member should be expected to make a subscription and pay it. It may be weekly, monthly, or quarterly, but it should be reliable and generous.

This enables the church to know how well its needs are provided for, and to "cut their coat according to the cloth." But the most important thing about it is the educative influence. The young folks, and even the children, should be taught by precept, by explanation, and by the example of their parents that churches must be supported; that ministers' families live on victuals, not on visions; that preachers' boys want coats, hats, and shoes; and preachers' girls want dresses and bonnets and gaiters. Children should never be allowed to hear complaints about the "cost of the church." But Sunday morning should be the time to "bring an offering" and "enter into his gates with thanksgiving, and into his courts with praise."

I have in my own pastorate seen little boys

begin their contributions, a few cents a week, delighted to be reckoned among the helpers; increase their amounts as their wages grew in size; then enter business for themselves, become prosperous, and give hundreds of dollars yearly, because the system itself, independent of any extraneous pressure, had educated them in their "reasonable service." The pew-renting system leaves it all with the father and he pays by check with no educational influence whatever. When he does this his sons are noncontributors.

I cannot speak too emphatically in urging the value of a system that educates the young for their work and responsibility. What is true of the support of the church at home applies with equal force to the system of providing for the missionary work. This should be a constant, not fluctuating system. But as we have seen in the chapter on motives it should have intelligent interest in the work of missionaries. That implies some sort of regular, interesting information to all the church about the Mission fields. The collection plate with no information makes a very feeble appeal to anybody. If we degenerate to the plane of simply *"making the budget"* it will soon rob us of any true partnership in the great undertaking of Christ.

Since these affairs are necessary to the spiritual interests of the church they are to be undertaken with prayer, and carried on with as fine an ethical spirit as the affairs of a revival meeting.

You will be asking how to bring about these conditions where they do not already exist.

A wise maxim is, " Never launch a ship until you have sounded the water to see if it is deep enough. Never try to cross a bar until you know the tide is full enough to carry your ship safely over."

Preach about your plan before you make any definite steps toward it. Turn conversation toward that subject when with your most loyal men. When the tide is high enough let your Advisory Committee, if you have one, talk it over. Avoid committing yourself to it so strongly that it will appear as a defeat of your wish if it does not meet with immediate approval. Be patient. Truth will win if it has time. Christian people see alike after they have thought things through. Thus your church will be a self-perpetuating school of method and munificence as well as a successful preaching platform.

XVII

From a babe thou hast known the sacred
writings, which are able to make thee wise
unto salvation, through faith which is in
Christ Jesus.—II Tim. 3:15.

EVANGELISTIC PEDAGOGY

THERE is a use of this word "evangelism"
to describe what has no relation to education. In that use it means sermons and agencies
that are immediately effective in getting people to
submit themselves to the Savior, and to openly
confess their faith. Such endeavors obtain results
with some people that never could be attained by
any other methods. For some people are so made
up that they cannot of themselves come to a
decision. They are like loaded guns, needing
something to fire them off; some percussion cap
to ignite their powder. Blessed is the man who
can be the cap for that service. I am not to discuss that kind of evangelism here.

But there is another use of the word to describe
in one word all the varied agencies and methods
that unite to bring people to a personal faith in
Jesus, but with special emphasis on the intellectual
element. It includes all forms of teaching Christian truth.

This part of the ministers' work is the more important for the reason that by far the greater part of all those who, in the past centuries as well as those in this present age, have come to their place in the church have come in a much less spectacular way than that which accompanies the first agency mentioned in this chapter.

This method to bring men to faith implies that truth is to reach the mind by the same channels that it comes in other departments of life. That is by gradual approaches, and finally by the compelling power of conviction as to duty and privilege. People cannot be educated *into* faith, but they can and must be educated *up to* it. The parable of the " Sower," as it is called as given in Matthew 13 reflects this truth. The seed is the word of the gospel; the soil is the human mind; the harvest is dependent on the condition of the soil. The minister now has a twofold work. He sows the seed, but he must also prepare the soil.

In this preparation of the soil some great facts must be recognized. *First,* there is a stage in the lives of all young folks in which they are simply taking in what is given them in unquestioning confidence. The lowest foundation-stones of their religion are laid at that time. The beginnings of an effective evangelism are made then. If a child gets an idea of God at that time which is chiefly characterized by his omniscience, and his holiness, and his severity; if he is one to stand afar off from and worship; if he inspires awe and perhaps fear it will affect their whole attitude toward religion in after years. One little girl sent her pet puppy back into the house when she was going out with the remark, " It is enough to have God tagging me around all the time without having you along." She had been made to think that omnipresence was the main characteristic of God. Another child had seen in the Sunday School room a great human eye painted on the wall above the teacher's desk. It was to him the chief characteristic of God that he could see all that is going on, and it was not agreeable to a boy who sometimes wanted to do things not right.

If there is one thing that is important for the minister to guard it is the influence he may be exerting on the minds of the young concerning the character of God and of Jesus. This is especially true in his prayers and his selections of hymns in public worship. To pray with a sense of awe, and with great high-sounding phrases, as if prayer was an exercise in rhetoric or an examination in theology, is almost sure to make the young afraid of God. The Roman Catholic system has that great weakness. The invocations of saints have the effect to make people think that Jesus is unapproachable directly. Some views of the atonement have the same effect in respect to

God.   Some hymns would scare an angel away
from the throne.

Jesus was not unapproachable.   The children
were not afraid of him.   The mothers brought
their children to him.   And if he was thus ap-
proachable then we have no reason to think that
now he has taken on so much dignity that we must
come tremblingly to him.   The writer of Hebrews
said, " Come boldly to a throne of grace, that we
may find mercy and grace to help in time of
need."

And Jesus' presentation of God is not under the
name of king or ruler or captain but Our Father
in heaven.   That word gathers up in one the
largest and loveliest conceptions of God that our
language can contain.   And that is the color of
the glass through which we are to look at him.

I am not saying that we are to talk to all children as " Jesus' little lambs " for they are not.
But we are to talk about him as the Good Shepherd of all his flock.

Secondly.   There comes another stage in child-
life when they begin to ask Why?   They are
animated interrogation marks.   Before we are
aware of it they are asking the great questions
of theology.   And they are quietly obtaining
their answers from what they hear in the pulpit.
There is a swift logic in the child's mind.   It is
said of a Chinese boy who was being taught Logic
that the teacher gave him these propositions and

asked him to give the conclusion: "All men are mortal." "The Emperor is a man." The boy replied, "Then he ought to repent right away." He jumped over the logical conclusion and went on in his own mind to another one drawn from the whole series.

The minister must make his sermons in some sense like the talk at one end of a telephone. It is one-sided to a listener. He must answer the questions his auditors are inwardly asking.

He must lead their minds over the course they need to follow in their thinking to a just conclusion. And especially lead them to a knowledge of those truths that are fundamental to any decision to become followers of Jesus. It will not do for him to dogmatize. He must indirectly reason. He must habitually give reasons for his statements. If you examine Paul's letters you will be greatly impressed by the frequency of the words "for" and "therefore." "For" generally gives the reason of a statement just preceding. An inquiring young man if he asked for the reasons of Paul's most positive statements would find them in the connection.

Thirdly. Then there comes a stage when the young will be asserting their individual independence—"individuating"—themselves. That is the time when they sit apart from the family pew, choose new companions, differ from their parents in many things, and especially decline to confer with the pastor about their religious thoughts. They are brooding over great things. It need give no great anxiety if the work has been well done before. This stage is a necessity. Faith must be personal. There is no second-hand faith possible. It is the greatest honor and the greatest responsibility that every individual soul has a place and a standing before God. " Every one must give account of himself to God." And hence every one must have his own faith toward God and toward him whom God hath sent.

There is a passage in John (8: 47) that has a very deep suggestion: " He that is of God heareth the words of God. For this cause ye hear them not, because ye are not of God."

What does he mean when he says, " Ye are not of God?" I think he means that they did not have any desire to know about God or to do as he wishes. Not having any such desire they would not see any worth in Jesus nor care about his words. But if there had been a deep desire to know God, a hunger in soul for his truth and his way of life, then Jesus' word would have been bread to them.

Therefore, giving people the right and winning idea of God so that they have a desire to know more of him is predetermining their reception of Jesus. It is so to speak loading the scales before they know it so that when the time comes for them to make their life choice of leadership they will not need to unlearn things they have imbibed about the Father in heaven before they can accept his Son. The minister who is thus teaching the young—the very young—and is encouraging the parents to thus teach, is doing the first things in true evangelism.

In this period when choice is to be made it will be made in accord with the deepest interests and moral tastes. But these tastes have been pre-determined by the earliest teachings about God, and about his Son. Such teaching is then a large part of the world's evangelism. And he who does it need not feel himself left out of the list of real harvesters in the Lord's field.

Printed in the United States of America

J. H. JOWETT, D.D. *Fifth Avenue Presbyterian Church New York*

The Whole Armour of God

12mo, cloth, net $1.35.

"This popular preacher is, not only by his own people, but also by large numbers of others, considered the very greatest preacher. He is possessed of a rare and perhaps unequalled combination of the very qualities which captivate. His thoughts are always expressed in the simplest possible diction, so that their crystalline clearness makes them at once apprehended."—*Christian Evangelist.*

EDGAR DE WITT JONES *Author of "The Inner Circle"*

The Wisdom of God's Fools

And Other Sermons. 12mo, cloth, net $1.15.

A volume of discourses, displaying the same facility for the right word and fitting phrase which marked the author's previous work. Mr. Jones preaches sermons that *read* well—a not at all common quality. He is a thinker too; and brings to his thinking a lucidity and attractiveness which make his presentation of great truths an artistic, as well as an inspiring achievement. A note of deep spirituality is everywhere manifest.

FREDERICK F. SHANNON *Pastor of the Reformed-Church-on-the-Heights, Brooklyn, N. Y.*

The Enchanted Universe

And Other Sermons. 12mo, cloth, net $1.00.

Mr. Shannon's reputation as an eloquent and forceful preacher is still further enhanced by his new volume of sermons. The fervid, glowing character of the popular Brooklyn pastor's appeals, make the reading of his latest book, not only an inspiring, but a fascinating exercise.

GEORGE W. TRUETT, D.D. *Pastor First Baptist Church, Dallas, Tex.*

We Would See Jesus and Other Sermons

Compiled and edited by J. B. Cranfill. Net $1.15.

"One of the greatest—many would say the greatest—of all the world's preachers to-day. It ranks high among the extant books of sermons, past and present, and deserves a place in millions of homes."—*Biblical Recorder.*

BISHOP CHARLES EDWARD CHENEY

A Neglected Power

And Other Sermons. 12mo, cloth, net $1.00.

"Thoroughly evangelical in spirit, refreshing in Biblical truth and abounding in helpful ministrations for every day life."—*Evangelical Messenger.*